PROPHETS, PERFORMANCE, AND POWER

Nancy,

Thanks for all the support on finance & treasuring—

You're a great colleague—

Bill

PROPHETS, PERFORMANCE, AND POWER

Performance Criticism of the Hebrew Bible

WILLIAM DOAN AND TERRY GILES

t&t clark

NEW YORK • LONDON

T & T Clark International, Madison Square Park, 15 East 26th Street, New York, NY 10010

T & T Clark International, The Tower Building, 11 York Road, London SE1 7NX

T & T Clark International is a Continuum imprint.

Cover art by William Doan

Cover design by Brenda Klinger

Library of Congress Cataloging-in-Publication Data

Doan, William, 1959-
Prophets, performance, and power : performance criticism of the Hebrew Bible / William Doan, Terry Giles.
p. cm.
Includes bibliographical references and index.
ISBN 0-567-02680-9 (pbk.)
1. Bible. O.T.—Prophets—Criticism, interpretation, etc. 2. Performance. 3. Bible. O.T. Amos—Criticism, interpretation, etc. I. Giles, Terry. II. Title.
BS1505.52.D63 2005
224'.06—dc22

2005006613

Printed in the United States of America

05 06 07 08 09 10 10 9 8 7 6 5 4 3 2 1

for Bonnie and Samantha Doan
and for Mom, Pat, and Karl

"There's a divinity that shapes our ends,
Rough-hew them how we will."
HAMLET V.II.10

for Bill and Rosa Giles

תפארת בנ ימ אבותם
The glory of children is their parents
PROV 17:6B

CONTENTS

FOREWORD

The Hebrew prophets spoke to their audiences. This one observation, almost too simple to even mention, is the basic premise of this book. And since the premise is so simple, if not painfully obvious, what could possibly occupy a whole book on its explanation? Just this: those prophetic words, first spoken, constituted a performance that began a remarkable journey, leading eventually to a corpus of literature quite distinct from the original and yet intimately dependent upon those first utterances. The prophetic performances communicated both imaginatively and cognitively. Embedded in the prophetic literature are echoes of that prophetic performance, now layered over by a scribal performance, that form the prophetic documents as we now know them. Performance criticism is a developing method of analysis that can help elucidate both the prophetic performances and the scribal presentation of those performances. In the pages that follow, we will explore those performance dynamics and attempt to understand more fully both the performance of the prophet and the way in which that performance was captured, rearranged, and even usurped by the scribal performer.

In one sense, what we are proposing in this book is neither new nor innovative. There have been many students of the Bible who have made mention of prophetic performances or dramas. Recently, some have advocated the acting out of Bible stories as a means of interpretation, and there is at least one book on the market that considers the Bible as a rich source of theatre. Although we appreciate these recent treatments of Bible and theatre, this kind of investigation is not really what we are about. We are not primarily interested in finding out if the prophets acted out much of what they had to say by means of dramatic skits (although undoubtedly they did act out a great deal). Neither are we interested in describing the rituals that the prophets may have borrowed from other social forums. Instead, we want to know how the prophets' ideas were communicated early on and how those ideas changed when they were eventually committed to writing.

In the pages that follow, we will seek to place the prophetic utterances into the context of performance criticism. We will examine the dynamics of performance—how a performer is granted social power and how that power operates on an audience. From there, we will look at the changes that take place when attempts to replicate a performance are made in the construction of a script and how some of those changes might be evidenced in the prophetic literature. Finally, we will think together about the relationship between the prophet and the scribe (playwright) and the codifying of the prophetic message. Our investigation will lead us to suggest that what once was considered a mutually beneficial relationship between the prophet and his disciples may in reality have been a struggle in which the prestige of the charismatic prophet-performer was usurped by the power of the pen.

The prophecy of Amos will serve as the focus of our performance criticism application. Throughout the book we will explore performance criticism ideas and structures, with the goal of enriching our understanding of the Amos document. Our intent is not to present an exhaustive treatment of Amos, but to contribute to a growing discussion about performance criticism by making concrete application to biblical studies.

Several questions will occupy our attention here:

- What is performance criticism, and how can it be used to aid in understanding biblical texts?
- What is a performative mode of thought, and how does it work in a preliterate setting?
- What is the relationship between the prophetic performer and the scribal performer?

- How does the transformation from an oral presentation to a literary presentation affect the conceptual discourse of the material?
- How does the medium transferability of oral discourse and written discourse affect audience dynamics in performance criticism?
- Can we apply this kind of investigation to the biblical prophecy of Amos as well as other portions of the Hebrew Bible?

Some of the material contained in the following pages has been developed over the past few years and tested out with colleagues from two different professional associations. We would like to express our gratitude to the members of the Eastern Great Lakes Biblical Society and to the members of the Comparative Drama Conference for their feedback, suggestions, and critiques. Whatever helpful insights may be contained in this book are in no small measure a result of the wonderful conversations we have been privileged to share with our colleagues from these two professional associations.

CHAPTER I

Prophets, Performance, and Power

This chapter and the next several chapters are about setting the stage. In this chapter, we begin to discuss those concepts that allow us to investigate prophets, performance, and power. We examine the oral nature of the prophetic presentation, posit performance as a type of orality, and then seek to understand what happens to orality when it appears in written texts.

Writing and Orality in the Hebrew Prophets

The first step in considering prophetic performance is simply to remind ourselves that many prophetic utterances were delivered orally. In her book *Oral World and Written Word*, Susan Niditch suggests, "It is possible that some works of the Hebrew Bible were composed in oral performance in accordance with certain conventions of composition, content, structure, and style."[1] What Niditch identifies as "conventions of composition, content, structure and style" will occupy our attention a little later. For now, it is enough to recognize that at least some of the material in the prophetic literature of the Hebrew Bible, now committed to writing, began its life as oral statements

1. Susan Niditch, *Oral World and Written Word* (Louisville, Ky.: Westminster John Knox, 1996), 117.

made by prophetic actors in front of attentive audiences.[2] Hermann Gunkel already noticed as much when he wrote: "They [the prophets] were originally orators, as can be seen from the expression 'Hear!' with which their speeches begin. We must try and imagine their sayings being uttered orally, and not as they stand on paper, if we are to understand them."[3]

Perhaps the most convenient place to survey the oral pronouncements made by the Hebrew prophets is in a set of books written by Claus Westermann: *Basic Forms of Prophetic Speech* and *Prophetic Oracles of Salvation in the Old Testament*.[4] In these two books, Westermann presents an impressive array of speech material found within the Hebrew prophetic literature and suggests a number of categories by which those speeches or oracles could be defined and analyzed. While extremely influential in the study of oracles within the prophetic literature, Westermann certainly does not represent the lone voice crying in the wilderness.[5] A quick survey of just a few of the many fine commentaries on the book of Amos shows that commentators have found the following: commission bound messenger speech, free witness speech, vision reports, funeral lamentation, oracles concerning the end,[6] speech

2. In some ways, what we are suggesting here has been offered before. See J. Herder, *The Spirit of Hebrew Poetry* (2 vols.; trans. J. Marsh; Burlington, Vt.: Edward Smith Publishers, 1833); and R. Lowth, *Lectures on the Sacred Poetry of the Hebrews* (trans. G. Gregory; London: Thomes Tegg & Son, 1835). Our contribution is to further the analysis of the previously recognized performance and suggest more precise terminology by which to analyze the performances of the prophets.

3. Hermann Gunkel, "The Israelite Prophecy from the Time of Amos," in *Twentieth Century Theology in the Making*, vol. 1, *Themes of Biblical Theology* (ed. J. Pelikan; trans. R. Wilson; New York: Harper & Row, 1969), 61.

4. See Claus Westermann, *Basic Forms of Prophetic Speech* (London: Lutterworth, 1967); Westermann, *Prophetic Oracles of Salvation in the Old Testament* (Louisville, Ky.: Westminster John Knox, 1991). See also David Peterson, "Basic Forms of Prophetic Literature," in *The Changing Face of Form Criticism for the Twenty-First Century* (ed. Marvin Sweeney and Ehud Ben Zvi; Grand Rapids: Eerdmans, 2003), 269–75. In this article, Peterson suggests the following five forms of prophetic literature: divinatory chronicle, vision report, prophetic speech, legend, and prophetic historiography.

5. Many examples could be cited, but perhaps only a few are needed to press home the point. John Barton has written a very helpful book on the Hebrew prophets, choosing to acknowledge the oral nature of the prophetic communication in the title: *Oracles of God* (Oxford: Oxford University Press, 1986). More recently, Ehud Ben Zvi and Michael Floyd have edited material from an ongoing consultation group of the Society of Biblical Literature that also recognizes the importance of investigating prophetic speech events. See Ehud Ben Zvi and Michael Floyd, eds., *Writings and Speech in Israelite and Ancient Near Eastern Prophecy* (Atlanta: Society of Biblical Literature, 2000).

6. See Hans Walter Wolff, *Joel and Amos* (trans. Waldemar Janzen, S. Dean McBride, and Charles Muenchow; Hermeneia; Philadelphia: Fortress, 1977).

against the nations[7] or, alternatively, oracles against the nations.[8]

But recognizing the oral origins of at least portions of the prophetic material is only half the story. Some of the prophets' oral performances were, in some fashion or other, transferred to writing, appearing then as literary pieces bearing the name of the orator. Writing is a function of social power, and the transformation of a prophetic oral pronouncement to a written one bearing the prophet's name involves the use of social power.[9] Scholars have addressed the social power of texts from a variety of vantage points. Philip Davies, in an article on the problem of canon, says that "writing transfers public knowledge from the people to the state."[10] Concerned with the social dimension of literacy, R. Pattison expresses the notion of the power of texts in this way: "Not every society has chosen to use literacy in the same way, but literacy is always connected with power."[11]

The relationship between writing and power exists on three levels: (1) power *over* texts, that is, power expressed in the production and distribution of a text; (2) power *through* texts, for example, through monumental inscriptions or their replacements and the consequent control of public access to knowledge; (3) and the power *of* texts, both in controversies that place the text at the focal point of social struggle and in controversies that use the text as a weapon of social power.[12] This last form of power is particularly relevant to

---

7. See John Hayes, *Amos, the Eighth-Century Prophet: His Time and His Preaching* (Nashville: Abingdon, 1988).

8. See Shalom Paul, *Amos* (Minneapolis: Fortress, 1991).

9. See the following excellent surveys: A. K. Bowman and Greg Woolf, eds., *Literacy and Power in the Ancient World* (Cambridge: Cambridge University Press, 1994); Brian Street, *Literacy in Theory and Practice* (Cambridge: Cambridge University Press, 1984); R. McKitterick, *The Uses of Literacy in Early Medieval Europe* (Cambridge: Cambridge University Press, 1990); and J. Humphry, *Literacy in the Roman World* (Ann Arbor, Mich.: University Press, 1991).

10. Philip Davies, "The Jewish Scriptural Canon in Cultural Perspective," in *The Canon Debate* (ed. Lee Martin McDonald and James Sanders; Peabody, Mass.: Hendrickson, 2002), 43. Even Davies, in the development of a model as an alternate to the oral composition model must concede that "the scrolls of Isaiah and Jeremiah, and also many of the 'Minor Prophets' (before their assemblage at some point onto a single scroll), do not really seem intended to be read for edification or pleasure—though we may have to reckon with the possibility of oral performance, perhaps in liturgical contexts." Davies, "Pen of Iron, Point of Diamond," in Ben Zvi and Floyd, *Writers and Speech in Israelite and Ancient Near Eastern Prophecy*, 75.

11. R. Pattison, *On Literacy: The Politics of the Word from Homer to the Age of Rock* (Oxford: Oxford University Press, 1982), viii.

12. A. Bowman and G. Woolf, "Literacy and Power in the Ancient World," in Bowman and Woolf, *Literacy and Power in the Ancient World*, 6–12.

sacred texts and to individuals or social groups that derive their status from the use or ownership of sacred texts. The process of transforming an oral prophetic performance into a text is an exercise of social power. The transformation takes ownership of the performance from the performer and gives it to the scribe. The transformation takes the performance from an oral audience and gives it to a much smaller group of literati. That this aspect of our investigation is necessary has been well illustrated by Ben Zvi: "Within a society in which the vast majority is illiterate and the total number of highly literate people is miniscule, the explicitly written character of particular instances of the word of YHWH—that is, the 'prophetic books' themselves—can not be considered a theological or literary feature of secondary importance."[13]

The transference to a written medium, according to Ben Zvi, "effectively creates a world in which YHWH's word is directly accessible only to a few literati in each generation."[14] These few "developed into absolutely necessary brokers of the knowledge of this divine word who alone could disseminate the teaching."[15] In other words, a performance, itself an exercise in social power, became a commodity of power when transformed into written texts.[16] But that act of writing required a new performance, and a new exercise of power, as the reader adopted the persona of the prophet to "perform" the written words that were uttered aloud and, in their hearing, once again became available to the nonliterate populace. Whether through the original prophetic speech or through the public reading of the prophetic text, both of which functioned as a call to hear the word of the Lord, a performance was enacted. The dynamics of performance helped create the medium in which the message was communicated. It is that medium to which we must now turn our attention.

PERFORMANCE MODE

What Susan Niditch characterizes as "certain conventions of composition,

13. Ehud Ben Zvi, "Introduction: Writings, Speeches, and the Prophetic Books—Setting an Agenda," in Ben Zvi and Floyd, *Writings and Speech in Israelite and Ancient Near Eastern Prophecy*, 8.

14. Ibid., 8.

15. Ibid., 10.

16. W. J. Ong, "Writing is a Technology that Restructures Thought," in Gerd Baumann, *The Written Word. Literacy in Transition* (Oxford: Oxford University Press, 1986), 23–50.

content, structure, and style" we label a *performance mode of thought,* in which oral performances were conveyed and compositional characteristics of which still reside embedded in the written literature. A performance mode of thought is that peculiar type of orality that is still evident in the prophetic literature of the Hebrew Bible. This will be identifiable through a performance criticism on the appropriate prophetic texts. While we disagree with Susan Niditch on how that orality was retained in the prophetic texts, we do think she is correct when she speculates, "If there are . . . written versions of oral performances in the Hebrew Bible, the poetry of the classical prophets seems a likely possibility."[17] These texts will be prime candidates for our performance criticism. Prior to that analysis, however, we must first consider just how any type of orality in texts manifests itself.

Linguistic Context of Orality in Texts

Linguists have spent considerable effort in investigating orality in written texts. Robert Cully, for example, provides a paradigm by which to think of the problem: "It is important to make a distinction between medium and conception, that is to say, whether a text is produced in an oral or written form (medium) and whether a text is conceived in oral or written terms (conception)."[18] He goes on to explain that in an

> oral-traditional setting, composition occurs using oral performance using the traditional idiom (orally conceived and orally presented). In contrast, we ourselves compose in writing because writing is "a way of organizing thought and text." . . . Orally derived texts would mean traditional texts conceived largely in oral terms but still produced in writing.[19]

Cully has made us aware of both the linguistic "medium" and the linguistic

17. Niditch, *Oral World and Written Word,* 120.

18. Robert Culley, "Orality and Writtenness in the Prophetic Texts," in Ben Zvi and Floyd, *Writings and Speech in Israelite and Ancient Near Eastern Prophecy,* 53.

19. Ibid., 53. The interaction of both conception and medium can be illustrated by observing Internet-savvy young people. While using a literary medium, they conceive the communication in a postliterate mode of thought. The resulting "text" is a strange mix of words and pictographs that follows a grammar and logic that can only be described as a composite residing somewhere between a written and oral form of communication.

"conception" of a communication. Wulf Oesterreicher confirms the necessary distinction of medium and conception when describing discourse: Orality as a "linguistic conception of discourse" is a "conceptional aspect of language" and "must be strictly differentiated from the medium aspect of language."[20] That is, there is a difference between the *linguistic medium* and the *linguistic conception*. Oesterreicher continues: "The conceptional profiles of any discourse are, as a matter of principle, independent of the medium of discourse."[21] The manner in which the conceptional profile and medium of exchange relate is more complex than a simple oral-literate continuum.[22] Oesterreicher stresses that the aspect of conception must be considered separately from the aspect of medium, for the two can operate independently of each other and are by no means of equal importance in analyzing the "oral/literate status of discourse."[23] Oesterreicher offers alternate labels for the orality-literacy continuum.[24] He suggests that the continuum is better

---

20. Wulf Oesterreicher, "Types of Orality in Text," in *Written Voices, Spoken Signs* (ed. Egbert Bakker and Ahuvia Kahane; Cambridge, Mass.: Harvard University Press, 1997), 191.

21. Ibid. See also Ludwig Soll, *Gesprochenes und geschriebenes Französisch* (Berlin: Schmidt, 1985); Michael Halliday, "Spoken and Written Modes of Meaning," and Wallace Chafe and Jane Danielewicz, "Properties of Spoken and Written Language," in *Comprehending Oral and Written Language* (ed. Rosiland Horowitz and S. Samuels; New York: Academic Press, 1987).

22. Oesterreicher, "Types of Orality in Text," 192–93, cites a basic paradigm of four quadrants: informal spoken, informal written, formal spoken, and formal written. This paradigm, he argues, is not sufficient to accurately describe the whole range of varieties present in human discourse, but it may be sufficient to help us identify performance characteristics.

23. Ibid., 193.

24. The notion of continuum is an important guard against an analysis that overly considers the differences between the oral and the written while neglecting the similarities that nonetheless exist between the two modes of communication. Jack Goody, *The Domestication of the Savage Mind* (Cambridge: Cambridge University Press, 1977), is often cited as an example of one who stresses the differences between orality and literacy. Brian Street provides a balancing position by calling attention to the socialization process in the construction of a literacy of any specific group. His argument against a "great divide" theory between orality and literacy is developed in an "ideological model." Street, *Literacy in Theory and Practice*, 95ff. Nevertheless, interesting empirical studies suggest there are different methods and mechanisms used by the brain to process information. One such study concludes that there is a "common substrate for the processing of incoming visual information and visual recall" (the mind's eye) that may accentuate the performative and nonperformative discursive differences. Gabriel Kreiman, Christof Koch, and Itzhak Fried, "Imagery Neurons in the Human Brain," *Nature* 408 (2000): 357–61. A similar argument is being debated over the way in which computer technology is changing the way people think. An interesting example is found in Sherry Turkle, "How Computers Change the Way We Think," *Chronicle of Higher Education* 50 (January 30, 2004): section B, 26–28.

described by the language of *immediacy* on the one hand, and the language of *distance* on the other.

To illustrate the ways in which the continuum might be observed in human interaction, Oesterreicher offers the following pairs of opposites:

- Face-to-face interaction of partners versus distance in space and time
- Private versus public setting of the communicative act
- Familiarity versus unfamiliarity in the partners
- Context embeddedness versus contextual dissociation of a discourse
- Dialogue versus monologue
- Maximum versus minimum cooperation of partners
- Spontaneity versus detachment
- Free topic versus fixed topic

The analysis that Oesterreicher and others suggest could be visually represented graphically in what we propose as a "variable discourse grid."

VARIABLE DISCOURSE GRID

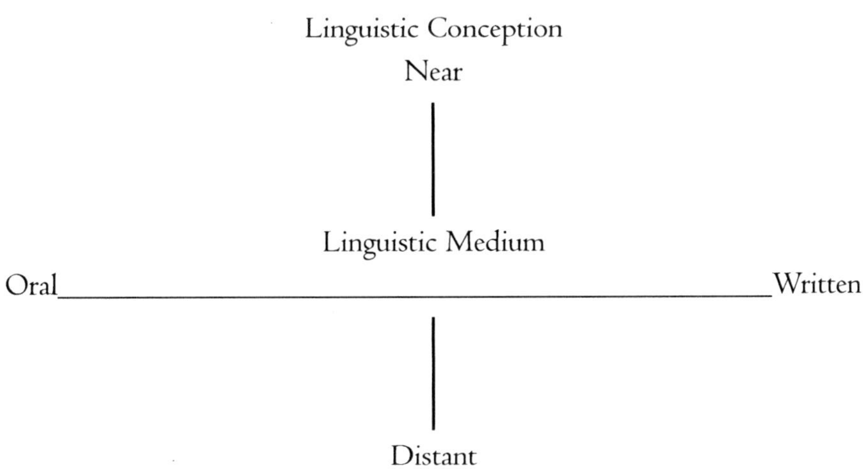

This graph, presenting four quadrants, shows how the conditions of communication can come together to create a communicative context. The communicative strategies of the speaker-writer will depend on the confluence of a number of the exemplary conditions discussed below.

VARIABLE DISCOURSE GRID

Linguistic Conception
Near

Face-to-face
Once used
Uses nonverbal communicative clue
Dialogue

Reusable
Relaxed
Experiential

Linguistic Medium
Oral______________________________Written

Distant

Monologue
Formal
Idea oriented

Permanent
Formal
Explanatory prose

This confluence combines to make the "conceptional profile of discourse."[25] *The discourse can be categorized,* for it tends also to conform to patterns recognized by the participants and implicitly agreed upon by the participants. *This implicit agreement allows the successful experience of communication.*[26]

Medium Transferability and "Twice-Used" Communication

The conceptual profile of a communication is not limited to one particular medium. An oral discourse can be transformed into a written discourse or vice versa. When the conceptional profile of a communication that is offered in one medium by the originator can be transferred to a second medium without affecting the "conceptual content of the discourse,"[27] that quality is referred to as "medium-transferability."[28] This is precisely the problem of orality in texts or, within the context of our interest in the Hebrew prophets, it is the problem of investigating prophetic oracles in the preserved prophetic literature. We must investigate the processes of medium-transferability that result in the presence of a performative mode of thought in a written text.[29]

Oesterreicher addresses this concern in the context of his own special interest by framing the question, "How can we recognize in the written documents the typical oral phenomena and the features of Latin varieties that represent communicative immediacy?"[30] We in turn would phrase the question like this: How can we recognize in the preserved documents of the Hebrew Bible the

25. Oesterreicher, "Types of Orality in Text," 194.

26. Oesterreicher offers the following as examples of the discourse traditions ranging from the immediate to the distant types: intimate conversation, telephone conversation with a friend, private letter, counseling, interview with a politician, sermon, university lecture, editorial, scientific article, legal contract. Oesterreicher, "Types of Orality in Text," 195. As building blocks contributing to the notion of a performative mode of thought, the conceptional profiles of discourse or the sets of preexisting traditions of discourse create the context for "performativity," or the perspective "from which the artist views the world in order to wrest from it its 'twice-behavedness.' An artist says, this is the way people behave N number of times, and knows how to put N into expressive form." Mikel Dufrenne, *The Phenomenology of Aesthetic Experience* (trans. Edward S. Casey et al.; Evanston, Ill.: Northwestern University Press, 1993), 13.

27. Oesterreicher, "Types of Orality in Text," 196.

28. John Lyons, *Language and Linguistics* (Cambridge: Cambridge University Press, 1981), 11.

29. The identification of "modes of thought" applied to oral and written communications is not original with us. Walter Ong uses the concept in *Orality and Literacy: The Technologizing of the Word.*

30. Oesterreicher, "Types of Orality in Text," 196.

typical oral phenomena associated with a performative mode of thought expressed in the immediacy of the prophetic speech events? Oesterreicher offers direction in answering that question: "In every linguistic community we can recognize a series of descriptive linguistic norms that regulate dialectical (diatopic), social (diastratic), and situational (diaphasic) differences. The totality of these different varieties constitutes what I call the variational space of a historical language."[31]

Since, however, we only have written texts from the linguistic community of the distant past, we are limited to a search for indirect evidence of the "traces or indications of conceptual orality."[32] This handicap should not dissuade the investigator. Oesterreicher again writes persuasively: "It is my conviction that not only linguistics but also in all disciplines dealing with texts the following question is long overdue: 'Why do linguistic elements, constructions, and procedures of the immediacy type occur in texts?'"[33] How is it that certain elements of oral discourse become "twice used" and find their way into written discourse as well?

Our goal is not just to determine the characteristics of speeches, oracles, and reports as they now find their way into the preserved prophetic literature. Rather, our concern is how do these speeches, oracles, and reports become twice used? What happens to the oral form of communication when it becomes transformed into a written form of communication? When this transformation takes place, who now controls the communication form and what social power does the communication now wield?

The first step is to define the characteristics of the performative mode of thought. The second step is to explore how it becomes twice used or how the medium transferability of this conceptional mode of discourse occurs. What happens to the performative mode of thought when it is presented in a text medium? Although prophetic actions and oracles are the objects of our investigation, it would be a mistake to be concerned only with actions and words. David Stacey offers a helpful reminder: "Plainly prophetic drama can not be understood apart from the whole complex of Hebrew thought."[34] It is that

31. Ibid., 198.

32. Ibid., 199.

33. Ibid.

34. David Stacey, *Prophetic Drama in the Old Testament* (London: Epworth, 1990), 11.

complex of Hebrew thought—expressed orally but preserved in writing—that forms the core of prophetic performance.

PERFORMANCE AS AN ASPECT OF ORALITY

The most effective means for arriving at definitions and for accomplishing the creation of a context for understanding the terms *performance, theatre,* and *drama* within the field of biblical studies is to take advantage of the "insider-outsider" categories that have emerged in the evolution of performance studies. For Bert States, a leading theorist in performance studies, the "outsider" theorists (e.g., Erving Goffman, Victor Turner) are those who can get outside the "thing," because they were never inside it as practitioners. "Insider" theorists (e.g., Richard Schechner, Peggy Phelan, Judith Butler) are those who either practice theatre production or theatre scholarship. States identifies Goffman and Turner as "complementary outsider-theorists who have fruitfully applied the theatre/performance metaphor, respectively, to the individual and to social life at large."[35] He continues:

> On the other extreme we have the insider-theorists, or people who are either theatre practitioners or theatre scholars, or, like Schechner, both: they come to performance study with a strong theatre orientation, and are therefore not so much making simple metaphorical connections as metonymical ones—that is, they are interested in extending the performance concept into contiguous fields of application (adjacent art forms, rituals, politics, and ceremonies of various kinds). . . . Unlike Goffman and Turner the insider-theorist's mission is now to define performance itself (not social behavior), and normally in the most basic possible terms.[36]

In establishing our notion of a performance mode of thought, it is not our intention to limit performance to the insider-theorist perspective. We are not addressing the question of how far a performance can go and still remain

35. Bert O. States, "Performance as Metaphor," *Theatre Journal* 48 (1996): 8.
36. Ibid., 8.

a performance, though we take advantage of how far the limits of performance have been pushed by the attempts of others to define the boundaries. States makes the point:

> Any specialized vocabulary or set of fixed terms does not exhaust the phenomenon it is intended to describe (performance, theatre, art) but simply "fixes" it from one possible angle of intentionality or expressiveness; for the phenomenon is always nameless and multiform before a vocabulary traps it in one of its manifestations. This is the reason we can never define a phenomenon like performance: its constitution is not the same as that of a machine, a disease or a molecule of water. It is a concept with "vague boundaries," as Wittgenstein says, that is permeable to new meanings. By the year 2010, the perfection of virtual reality alone will have added unheard of dimensions to the field of performance. We can only seek the essential nature of performability, not a taxonomy of performable objects or behaviors.[37]

Summarizing his argument for performance as metaphor, States argues that performance depends on three phases: "It begins in the natural (or twice-behaved) behavior of Goffman's and Turner's 'raw' society or nature, gets refined in Schechner's composition or rehearsal process, and it is completed in Phelan's interaction of the work and the spectator who 'already understands' what the work is about, having lived it in one way or another."[38]

By resisting traditional definitions, boundaries, and conclusions, the protean nature of performance and performance theory reminds us of several of its key characteristics, particularly in relationship to theatre and theatrical analysis. Human activity is the medium of theatre, both in life and on the stage. Patterns of human activity are perceived through isolation in time and space. These patterns of activity are reinforced, changed, and adjusted by a wide range of forces from within and without any individual culture. The patterns of activity are performed and re-performed, but with a self-

37. Ibid., 20.
38. Ibid.

consciousness on the part of the performers and the spectators. In the case of the prophetic text, this "self-consciousness" arises from the oral tradition of both the prophets themselves and the written tradition of the scribes that preserves and alters that tradition. In other words, the performability of the prophetic tradition emerges from the ways in which the prophetic activity, the oral tradition, and the written tradition permeate each other.

The movement from oral to written is not a simple process between two poles of a dichotomy.[39] The same is true of movement between modes of thought. The performance mode of thought must first be situated within the problem of defining performance. In his introduction to a special issue of the *Drama Review* in 1973, Richard Schechner outlined seven areas of intersection between performance theory and the social sciences, five of which also intersect with the recent conversation in the literature on Bible and theatre:

1. Performance in everyday life, including gatherings of every kind.
2. The structure of sports, ritual, play, and public political behavior.
3. Analysis of various modes of communication (other than the written word); semiotics.
4. Connections with human and animal behavior patterns with an emphasis on play and ritualized behavior.
5. Ethnography and prehistory, both of exotic and familiar cultures.[40]

Those familiar with the prophetic literature will find a strange familiarity in these five characteristics.[41]

---

39. For a helpful summary of a complex process, see Michael Floyd "'Write the Revelation!' (Hab 2:2): Re-imagining the Cultural History of Prophecy," in Ben Zvi and Floyd, *Writings and Speech in Israelite and Ancient Near Eastern Prophecy*, 103–43.

40. Richard Schechner, "Drama, Script, Theatre and Performance," *Drama Review* 17 (1973): 5.

41. Compare this with descriptions offered by other biblical scholars. Robert Wilson, "Prophets and Ecstasy: A Reexamination," *Journal of Biblical Literature* 98 (1979): 324–37, considers the ecstatic nature of prophecy and concludes, "The question of prophecy and ecstasy is far more complex than earlier scholars had supposed" (337). Abraham Heschel prefers to call the prophetic state a "divine pathos" that led the prophet into a deeper understanding of the reality of God. Abraham Heschel, *The Prophets* (New York: Harper & Row, 1962), 2:11. J. Lindblom, too, is aware of a participation in a "mental state of intense inspiration" that came over the prophets directing their words and actions. J. Lindblom, *Prophecy in Ancient Israel* (Philadelphia: Fortress, 1962), 46. Regardless of the origin of this mental or ecstatic state, our contention is that it constituted a performance.

PERFORMANCE DEFINED

The term *performance*, writes Marvin Carlson, "is heavily indebted to terminology and theoretical strategies developed during the 1960s and 1970s in the social sciences, and particularly in anthropology and sociology."[42] As Carlson points out, critical writings that connect across the boundaries of theatre, anthropology, and sociology by Richard Schechner, Victor Turner, Erving Goffman, Dwight Conquergood, Peggy Phelan, and Julia Kristeva, among others, have created an expanding framework for performance theory that has, over time, demonstrated the fluid nature of the relationship between performance and text as well as between performance and life. Richard Bauman defines performance as "a consciousness of doubleness, through which the actual execution of an action is placed in mental comparison with a potential, an ideal, or a remembered model of that action."[43] Current thinking about performance and performativity, whether in theatre and performance studies, the social sciences, or linguistics, is a sprawling dialogue that ranges from explaining all human behavior as performance to a more narrowly focused notion of performance as "restored behavior." Richard Schechner describes at length the idea of restored behavior:

> Restored behavior is living behavior treated as a film director treats a strip of film. These strips of behavior can be rearranged or reconstructed; they are independent of the causal systems (social, psychological, technological) that brought them into existence. They have a life of their own. The original "truth" or "source" of the behavior may be lost, ignored, or contradicted—even while this truth or source is being honored and observed. How the strip of behavior was made, found, or developed may be unknown or concealed; elaborated; distorted by myth and tradition. . . . Restored behavior is used in all kinds of performances from shamanism and exorcism to trance, from ritual to aesthetic dance and theatre, from initiation rites to social dramas, from psychoanalysis to psychodrama and transac-

---

42. Marvin Carlson, *Performance: A Critical Introduction* (New York: Routledge, 2003), 14.
43. Cited in Carlson, *Performance*, 5.

> tional analysis. In fact, restored behavior is the main characteristic of performance.[44]

Critical to this notion of restored behavior is Schechner's recognition that practitioners of all kinds of performance (in our case, the scribes) assume that some behaviors ("organized sequences of events, scripted actions, known texts"[45]) and oral traditions are separate from the performer and can be "stored, manipulated, transmitted, and transformed."[46] Restored behavior is both symbolic and reflexive; it is "the hardening into theatre of social, religious, aesthetic, medical and educational process."[47] It is in this problem of restored or twice-behaved behavior that Schechner positions himself on the inside of theatre practice, as opposed to Goffman, who believes that performances do not restore anything, but simply occur. This boundary line, between theatre practice (making theatre as art) and the metaphoric framework of *life as a performance,* is actually the space we are traversing by suggesting the concept of a performance mode of thought. As Schechner observes: "Established genres are about performances that have found their place. Performative activities, on the other hand, are 'processual' by nature. They are in the process of transformation and are categorically indefinable."[48] The scribes were processing the lives and the acts of the prophets, creating a performance space on the written page, and contributing to the spectator/performer aggregate. The fluid nature of performance allows us to use the theatre as a hermeneutical tool for isolating elements of the theatre and drama in the Hebrew Bible while at the same time making metonymical connections between theatre practice and prophetic function.

Yet it is not a straight line from prophetic performance to literate recoding of that performance. The process of recording can change and even undermine the original performative intent of the prophet. Marvin Carlson points out how performance can work to undermine tradition and to provide a "site for the exploration of fresh and alternative structures and patterns of

44. Richard Schechner, *Between Theatre and Anthropology* (Philadelphia: University of Pennsylvania Press, 1985), 35. In this second chapter of the book, Schechner develops an elaborate model for examining the "twiceness" of behavior.

45. Ibid., 36.

46. Ibid.

47. Ibid.

48. Ibid., 118.

behavior."[49] This raises the question of whether performance serves to reinforce the primary assumptions and values of a culture, or to create new or alternative assumptions. Not only are we faced with the problematic question of what performance is, but also what performance accomplishes and how it accomplishes what it does for all participants. After completing his extensive study of approaches to the problem of performance, Carlson writes, "Performance by its nature resists conclusions, just as it resists the sort of definitions, boundaries, and limits so useful to traditional academic writing and academic structures."[50]

In other words, performance always carries with it a subversive potential. It has the ability to recreate and re-form the everyday and ordinary into something quite unexpected. Performance, Bert O. States reminds us, is a multifeatured concept "in which we slide from one manifestation of the phenomenon to another (e.g., from theatre to ritual, from ritual to parade, from parade to protest . . . etc.)"[51] This sliding can gradually make things seem more different than they are alike. However, as one moves across the continuum of performance, there are certain features, or "family resemblances," that make them continually open to metaphorical extension.[52] In essence, as one moves across this continuum, whether from a sociological, anthropological, linguistic, or artistic point of view, one is identifying a variety of performances and performance modes. Whether it is a performance (e.g., parade, protest, Broadway production) or performative (e.g., the presentation of the self in one's social life), the metaphor has expanded to include everything in the given semantic network.[53]

Regarding performance, Bernard Beckerman writes, "Performance alerts us to what the performer does; it contains the idea of process and hints at the changing nature of what is performed."[54] In all kinds of performance, the idea, the fundamental structure of what is performed, remains "communally

---

49. Carlson, *Performance*, 15.

50. Ibid., 189.

51. States, "Performance as Metaphor," 3.

52. Ibid.

53. States provides a concise semantic history of the word *performance* and suggests, using Raymond Williams and Umberto Eco, that any word is "subject to tropological drift," or Eco's Pelican effect (ibid., 1–4).

54. Bernard Beckerman, *Theatrical Presentation: Performer, Audience, and Act* (ed. Gloria Brim Beckerman and William Coco; New York: Routledge, 1990), 1.

produced, dependent on tradition, and comprehensible only as a social effort."[55] With very few exceptions, all presentational acts are part of a heritage, part of the continuation of a presentational idea. This is certainly true in the case of prophetic literature. We suggest that the prophetic text is an analogue of the performance of the prophets, part of a continuing rendition that is part of a presentational idea. What is preserved in the prophetic text is a generalized pattern belonging to the *acts* of the *prophet*. The scribes, by preserving the act itself as well as the tradition of the act, were abstracting it, or operating in a performance mode of thought by preserving the following:

- the phenomenal: the act itself
- the schematic: the structure of the act
- the conceptual: what the act signifies

In other words, as we move from the prophets themselves, to the sons of the prophets, to the scribes and the creation of the prophetic text, we witness a continuity of performance, preserved through orality, repetition of the tradition, and the creation of the text, or script, through which the pattern of prophetic performance is preserved. The act, or pattern of prophetic performance, not only includes the separate manifestations of the original prophetic behaviors and messages but also the continuation of that tradition by others and the preservation of that tradition by scribes; the essential idea is the core element of the continuum. The essential idea, writes Beckerman, is not "a discursive concept but a structural principle that makes the act potentially exciting."[56] What could be more exciting and provocative than calling others to hear the word of the Lord?

55. Ibid., 8.
56. Ibid., 11.

CHAPTER TWO

From the Prophetic Performer to the Scribal Performer

In the last chapter, we made the case for thinking about the Hebrew prophets under the rubric of performance. We suggested that their oral pronouncements were performances and that performance criticism can help us understand the dynamics of the prophetic presentations. Further, and with the assistance of linguistic theory and research, we posited the presence of a performative mode of thought still embedded in the prophetic literature. In this chapter, we extend the line of investigation into the prophetic literature itself. Specifically, we turn our attention to the role of the scribe responsible for the creation of the prophetic literature. We investigate the relationship of the prophet to the scribe and ask questions concerning the social power struggle between the two.

THE PROPHET AND THE SCRIBE

Scribe versus Prophetic Performer

One of the tenets of conventional wisdom concerning the formation of the prophetic literature of the Hebrew Bible is that the literature was created from preserved traditions about the prophets kept alive by their disciples.

Presumably, a prophet, through his own charisma, the status of his social position, or the attractiveness of his message, was able to gather around himself a "school" or group of disciples that became committed to preserving the message and social vision of the prophet long after the prophet himself was forced to put aside his prophetic mantel.[1] Thus, traditional readings of the prophets have assumed that the transformation from prophetic utterance to prophetic literature was smooth and peaceful as the disciples honored their master by preserving traditions and sayings attributed to him. The disciples sought to be faithful to their prophetic master, even if the literature they created required that the original material be reworked and altered here and there in order to make it compatible to the new social and political context in which the disciples lived. Conventional wisdom said that in the prophetic literature, the disciples sought to "re-present" their master in the centuries following his death. In terms of social power, the process was thought to be a relatively uneventful transformation of power from the charisma of the prophet to the pen of the scribe.

Recently, however, some have questioned this conventional wisdom. Philip Davies has made his doubts quite clear: "The view that the prophets had disciples who preserved and updated the sayings of their masters has never been supported by anthropological or literary evidence; it merely supplies a convenient mechanism whereby these edited compositions can be traced back to an individual prophet."[2]

Davies observes that if the prophetic literature, particularly the Minor Prophets, was intended to honor prophetic masters, it is strange that it contains so few references to the "historical context, the life and the deeds" of the prophets that were being honored.[3] Leaving aside Jonah, of the twelve, only the books of Amos, Haggai, and perhaps Hosea have any narratives about the prophet. Amos and Hosea are presented as contemporaries but never find mention in one another's book. Even the superscriptions in which the

1. See William R. Harper, *A Critical and Exegetical Commentary on Hosea and Amos* (Edinburgh: T&T Clark, 1905); Hans Walter Wolff, *Joel and Amos* (trans. Waldemar Janzen, S. Dean McBride, and Charles Muenchow; Hermeneia; Philadelphia: Fortress, 1977); James Luther Mays, *Amos* (Philadelphia: Westminster, 1969); and Jorg Jeremias, *The Book of Amos* (trans. Douglas Scott; Louisville, Ky.: Westminster John Knox, 1998).

2. Philip Davies, *Scribes and Schools: The Canonization of the Hebrew Scriptures* (Louisville, Ky.: Westminster John Knox, 1998), 118.

3. Ibid., 117.

honored prophet is mentioned, and from which each book now derives its name, may be "guesswork."[4]

Guesswork or not is hard to prove. But we agree that the relationship between the prophet and a presumptive "school" is still unclear. The identity, role, and function of the "disciples of the prophets" deserve further investigation, and performance criticism provides anthropological tools by which to pursue the inquiry. A performance analysis of the prophetic event and literature suggests that the relationship between the two is analogous to the relationship between a performer and a script. The prophet is a performer who exercises social power through the immediacy of the performance. The message and delivery come together in the person of the prophet. A skillful performance by the prophet effectively holds sway over the audience by impacting upon them the correctness of the prophet's point of view. In the moment of performance, the prophet is not only a messenger but is the personification of the message. The message has power because the prophet has power.[5]

But this melding together of message and messenger is fleeting. It has no staying power because the prophet, the messenger, is transitory. Permanence can be achieved only through replication, only through a script that, when read, allows others to approximate the role of the messenger. Permanence can be achieved only by usurping the role of the prophet. And this is where tension results. Rather than a smooth transition from prophet to literature, it is much more likely that the evolution from prophetic performer to prophetic literature was characterized by a struggle for power. The prophetic scribe (or, perhaps better, the prophetic playwright) is dependent upon the prophetic performer for his inspiration and derives his credibility from an attachment to the prophetic performer but, nonetheless, is bent on replacing the prophetic performer. Whether intentional or not, the effect of the literature is to script the prophetic performance and in so doing to control the

4. Ibid., 118.

5. Julius Wellhausen spoke eloquently to this: "It belongs to the notion of prophecy, of true revelation, that Jehovah, overlooking all media of ordinances and institutions, communicates Himself to the *individual*, the called one, in whom that mysterious and irreducible rapport in which the deity stands with man clothes itself with energy. Apart from the prophet, *in abstracto*, there is no revelation; it lives in his divine-human ego." Wellhausen, *Prolegomena to the History of Israel* (Edinburgh: A&C Black, 1885), 398.

prophetic performance. The writer of the script can only exist as a replacement to the prophetic performer and cannot afford an encore performance by the prophet. Therefore, a future outbreak of the prophetic spirit is met with the darkest of warnings (Zech 13:1–6).

The prophet, on the other hand, just like any performer, is resistant to the imposition of limitations that a script represents. In the performance, the performer reserves for himself the ownership of the message. The prophetic performer admonishes his audience to *hear* the word of the Lord—rarely to *read* it.

Power in Texts

There are already recognized parallels to the transformation between oral and written discourse that we are suggesting here. Although not within the context of a performance, others have commented upon the power struggle that persists in the transition from an oral tradition to a written one. James Crenshaw has put together a cogent argument for the transformation of oral transmission to written within the educational traditions of ancient Israel that may be analogous to a prophetic performance dynamic.[6] He contends that the transformation of an oral tradition to a written text is a significant event, one that converged several lines of social power. He writes: "Sparsely populated villages had little need for literate persons, and the scribal guild zealously guarded its monopoly on writing. In such an oral culture, written words (icons) *shimmered with the power of the sacred,* and religious figures used popular awe to their own advantage."[7]

But the act of committing the performance to writing invokes a new social power. Crenshaw describes this transformation by quoting a Yoruba proverb: "The white man who created writing also created the eraser."[8] The master of the written medium is also master of the tradition committed to writing. And control of that tradition may not have been surrendered willingly or happily.[9]

6. See James Crenshaw, *Education in Ancient Israel* (New York: Doubleday, 1998).

7. James Crenshaw, "Transmitting Prophecy across Generations," in *Writings and Speech in Israelite and Ancient Near Eastern Prophecy* (ed. Ehud Ben Zvi and Michael Floyd; Atlanta: Society of Biblical Literature, 2000), 41 (italics ours).

8. Ibid., 43.

9. We are reminded of a colleague who characterizes computers as simply "fancy typewriters." In his disparagement of electronic communication he is actually expressing frustration over his loss of control of information that is the result of his lack of ability in navigating the new and, for him, unfamiliar medium.

The dynamic of power and control over the written medium is altogether different than the dynamic at work in an oral medium, for as Crenshaw again observes, "A written text can not choose its readers,"[10] while a speaker can choose to whom he speaks. Once put into writing, the tradition is subject to the manipulation of the literate, and the rest of the oral population must now rely upon the literate as the intermediary guardian and dispenser of the power of the tradition.

At this point, we should mention a fascinating characteristic of the way in which the prophets are depicted in the Hebrew Bible. With rare exception, the prophets have no closure. Unlike the biblical portrayal of kings or other significant community figures, who died and slept with the fathers, or who are given some other statement of finality, there is no such conclusion to the lives of most of the prophets. They do not die, ride off into the sunset (excepting Elijah), or live happily ever after. They are open ended. Even those whose ends are recorded are presented in a way that prevents closure. Moses is secreted off by God and, although mourned by the community, his burial spot is known only to God. Yet Mosaic prophecy does not end, and it becomes a hope for the community (Deut 18:18–20). Likewise, the previously mentioned Elijah may make a dramatic exit in the fiery chariot, but his mantle falls to Elisha, who continues in the Elijah tradition (2 Kgs 2:19–24). It is this same Elijah whose return is expected (Mal 4:5).

From Prophetic Actor to Prophetic Character

The point to be made is this: The prophets find no conclusion because the scribes writing the prophetic literature will not allow them to conclude. The scribes create prophetic *characters* out of the prophets themselves (prophetic *actors*).[11] The character continues long after the actor has left the scene. Yet, even though the scribes create and preserve the character of the prophet, the scribes are not interested in the resumption of prophecy itself.

10. Crenshaw, "Transmitting Prophecy across Generations," 43.

11. The character of the prophet, or the way in which the prophetic persona is depicted in the prophetic literature, is recognized by a growing number of biblical scholars. See, for instance, A. G. Auld, "Prophets through the Looking Glass: Between Writings and Moses," *Journal for the Study of the Old Testament* 27 (1983): 3–23; and E. Conrad, "The End of Prophecy and the Appearance of Angels/Messengers in the Book of the Twelve," *Journal for the Study of the Old Testament* 73 (1997): 65–79.

Prophecy reaches a conclusion (Zech 13:4–6) even if the prophetic character continues. The difference between character and actor resides at the crux of the struggle for power and control between the prophet and the scribe.[12] That difference can only be found in the performance itself. In the case of the prophet, his playwright was God, and the words he took from the lips of God made him a prophet. So how do we explain the relationship between the prophet as person and the prophet as character? What is that relationship between actor and character over which the scribe needed to gain control? According to Bert States, the question is "How does the actor speak to the audience about the character he is playing?"[13]

> Immediately we see that the I of the actor is not at all the I of the character he is playing, the voice that keeps saying, "I, I, I" throughout the play. The actor's first person is what appears before us as the character, the being that has, in effect, no voice of its own but whose very presence and way of appearing constitute the act of direct speech within the indirect speech in the enacted event. It is visible in the effortless hard work that produces on the actor's brow beads of perspiration that do not belong to the character. But the I is not simply the actor's real body. It is rather the unnatural attitude of the body, the thousand different means and behavioral peculiarities by which the actor unavoidably remains just outside the character he is playing.[14]

By appropriating the character of the prophet, the scribe became, both in speaking and writing the prophetic text, what appeared before his spectators *as* the character of the prophet.

To illustrate this process, we offer the following graphic image, which establishes a visual representation of the prophetic performance as an enacted event. Since we will focus on the book of Amos in the chapters that follow,

12. James Linville goes as far as saying that, in the prophetic book that bears his name, "Amos becomes redundant and loses his presence in the text." Linville, "Visions and Voices: Amos 7–9," *Biblica* 80 (1999): 23.

13. Bert O. States, *Great Reckonings in Little Rooms: On the Phenomenology of Theatre* (Berkeley: University of California Press, 1985), 124.

14. Ibid., 124–25.

we have used Amos the shepherd/prophet as the example in the graph. The graph also visualizes the central problem: There was a prophetic tradition tied to the actual lives of the prophets that ended in a scribal or written tradition that no longer had the presence of the prophet as the primary medium of the presentation. As the graph demonstrates, Amos the shepherd becomes Amos the prophet as a result of being called by God. His power comes from that fact. When he performs as prophet, he is able to bring God before his spectators. The scribe, in order to create the drama of Amos, has to appropriate Amos the prophet, both in his writing and reading of the text, if he is to achieve the power of the prophet.

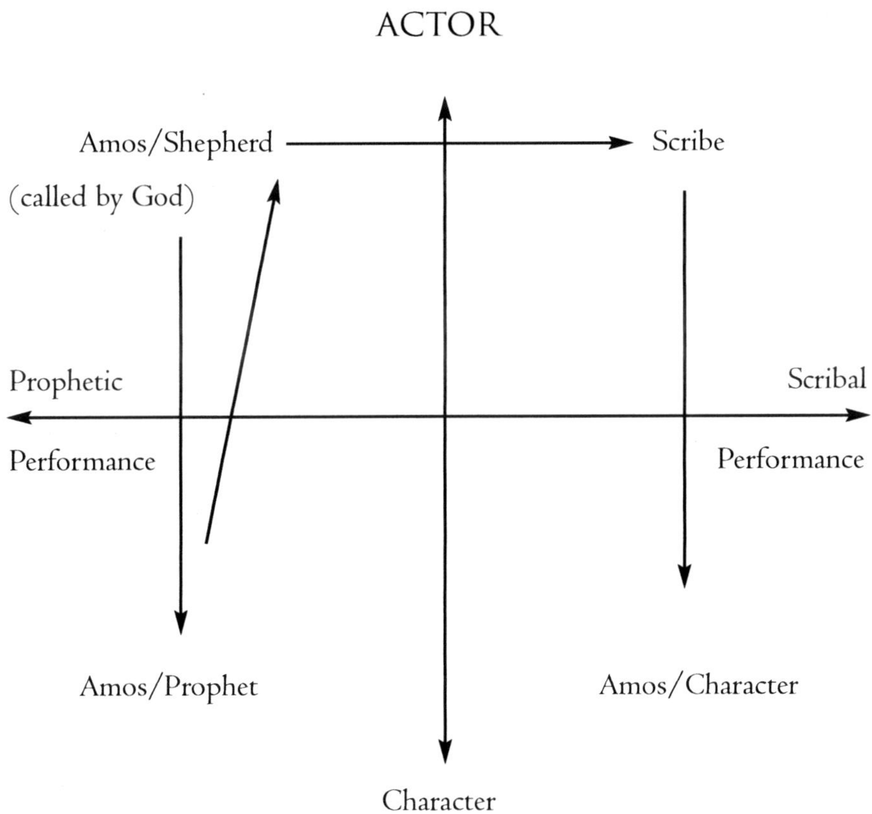

Presentational versus Literary

There is a fundamental conflict between the literary and the presentational mind. Though they did not cast the distinction in these terms, both Plato and Aristotle made a sharp distinction between the poet speaking in his own voice and speaking through the characters. Plato saw this distinction as fundamental. For him, the poet speaking through others was creating a lie, providing a pale imitation of an imitation. In his own voice, at least, the poet kept close to the truth. "Aristotle did not hold the same moral position regarding the distinction, but he did recognize it as an aesthetic matter and sought to describe the peculiar features of the dramatic mode. The effect has been to mute the critical conflict between the literary and the presentational mind."[15]

The conflict here is between control and point of view. We must remember that material meant to be presented is not necessarily connected by style or theme, "but by the idea of common presentation."[16] In the history of presentation, we find the full range of performances, from some that went on for days to performances that lasted under an hour. For example, a presentation of the medieval Wakefield Cycle plays probably began around 4:30 a.m. and ended at sunset, with potentially thirty-two plays being presented on wagons moving from station to station throughout town.[17] Each of the plays constituted an "act," but only the whole series constituted the show. And though the cycle plays were thematically linked, the variety of modes of presentation—in terms of spoken vernacular, use of comedy, farce, and specific skill—was a loose connection of choices determined by the local guild responsible for each individual act. The power was in the hands of the performer, who controlled the spectator's relationship to the act not only by *what* was performed but also by *how* it was performed.

As Beckerman writes, "If we follow Plato's line of reasoning, the poet speaking in his own voice maintains his own point of view. He shapes his emotion or thought in the lyric and his narrative in the epic to express a consistency of outlook, a consistency over which he can exert control if he

---

15. Bernard Beckerman, *Theatrical Presentation: Performer, Audience, and Act* (ed. Gloria Brim Beckerman and William Coco; New York: Routledge, 1990), 91.

16. Ibid., 89.

17. The Wakefield Cycle plays were medieval dramas that dealt specifically with biblical themes. They were performed on wagons that traveled from town to town. Each wagon presented one play in the multiplay cycle.

wishes. The result is that a literary work, in its very being, tends toward coherence. But when the poet allows his characters to speak in their own voices, he has to attain an objectivity or effect a disappearance so that the characters seem to be autonomous creatures." Moreover, conceived as a show, that independence is magnified by the fact that the roles of the characters are assumed by actual human beings, performers with their own identities. To this, one must add the fact that the process of creating sustained attention in performance is very difficult. "The same meter or the same subject, continued at moderate length, seems interminable. The need for variety makes itself felt. Consequently, the autonomy of the performing elements, together with the constant change required to hold an audience's attention, undermine many of the values so dear to the writer." Conventions appropriate in the structure of the performative mode may not be appropriate in a literary presentation. "Only a writer who is knowledgeable, cunning, and imaginative can devise a subterranean control over work that is intended for show."[18]

From a literary perspective, the performative mind has an inherent resistance to the unitary point of view.[19] The performative mind is keenly aware that it must juggle the twin demands of variety and intensification in order to move the work forward and to keep spectators engaged. Unity is derived more from performative structures such as voice modulation, gesture, proximity to spectators, pauses, and rhythms of movement than from the narrative of a text. The scribes, who were creating text that still had to be spoken and performed for the majority of their audience, sought to capture the performative mind and imagination of the prophet. The prophet, in the act of performing as prophet, was the medium through which God appeared. The scribe, both as writer and speaker of the text, engaged in a kind of impersonation. This brings us to the point of theatrical analysis. From a phenomenological perspective, the question becomes, "What kind of being would choose impersonation as a means of securing any advantage?"[20]

> Surely theatre's origins and purposes are not exhausted in the idea that man wants to imitate the world, as it is or as it

18. Beckerman, *Theatrical Presentation*, 91.

19. Ibid.

20. States, *Great Reckonings in Little Rooms*, 2. This question is different from the usual historical inquiry into the origins of theatre. It has particular value here since the scribes were engaged in both an impersonation of and a re-creation of the prophets.

> should be, or to make the crops do his bidding, or to honor the gods, or simply to entertain his fellow man, if by that we mean offering fictions about his social and private life. If the impersonation has the power to do these things, then the power itself must be prior to and independent of them. . . . It remains beneath all purposes an assertion of a certain power to create, to bring forth.[21]

This is precisely the power the prophets themselves had, that is, the power to bring forth the presence of God. In discussing a phenomenological approach to understanding the theatre, States relies on both Hegel and Heidegger as a way of reaching beyond the Aristotelian problem of mimesis and imitation.[22] Both Hegel and Heidegger are useful here because they address not only the question of why a being would choose impersonation as a means for securing advantage but also the seriousness of the imaginary, or illusory, world of the object created. As Heidegger explains:

> [The sculpture] is not a portrait whose purpose is to make it easier to realize how the god looks; rather, it is a work that lets the god himself be present and thus *is* the god himself. The same holds for the linguistic work. In tragedy nothing is staged or displayed theatrically, but the battle of the new gods against the old is being fought. The linguistic work, originating in the speech of the people, does not refer to this battle; it transforms the people's saying so that now every living word fights the battle and puts up for decision what is holy and what unholy, what great and what small, what brave and what cowardly, what lofty and what flighty, what master and what slave.[23]

---

21. Ibid.

22. As States argues in the introduction to *Great Reckonings in Little Rooms*, "The longstanding problem of mimetic theory is that it is obliged to define art in terms of what it is not, to seek a source of artistic representation in the subject matter of art, and to point to a place where it can be found, if only in a set of abstract ideas or truths, or in some field of essences or archetypes." *Action*, however, refers to something inside the play, perhaps even a "soul," or "indwelling form" (5–7).

23. Martin Heidegger, *Poetry, Language, Thought* (trans. Albert Hofstadter; New York: Harper & Row, 1975), 46–47; quoted in States, *Great Reckonings in Little Rooms*, 2.

In the prophetic tradition, it was the prophet through whom God himself was present. In the scribal tradition, it was the scribe who, as actor, *created* the character of the prophet in order for God to be present. The prophet brought the truth of God onto the stage, whether it was on a threshing floor, standing on a wall, or amidst a crowd gathered in the street. "It is the truth of the god that arrives on the stage and not the stage that refers to a real god beyond it, existing in some unavailable form."[24] Hegel's explanation of this phenomenon is that "[the gods] are made, invented, but are not fictitious. They certainly come forth out of the human imagination in contrast to what actually exists, but they do this as *essential* forms, and this product of the mind is at the same time recognized as being what is essential."[25]

What Hegel and Heidegger are both talking about is a principle of presence, which is different from a referential principle as the basis of art. The prophet *himself* was the presence through which God appeared to the people of Israel. This was more than a linguistic moment; it was a moment of full sensory engagement for both the prophet and the spectators. The scribe, both as writer and speaker of the prophetic text, cannot create that moment. He must impersonate the prophet, by creating the prophetic character, in order to create the illusion of the prophetic experience. In this sense he creates the prophetic drama. He impersonates the prophet in order to bring forth the presence of the prophet, which will bring forth the presence of God. Though the scribe writes, "Thus says the LORD," his words are meant to be spoken and heard; the prophet is brought forth so that God can be made present. In doing so, the scribe has appropriated the prophet's power to create. The scribe is simultaneously the creator and the actor of the text. The prophet is now a character, portrayed by the scribal actor. The drama no longer belongs to the prophet; it is now under control of the scribe.

The transition from performer to playwright as the primary power figure in establishing the tradition of tragedy is as much the study of a sociocultural shift of power as an aesthetic one. As Beckerman points out about ancient Greece, the modes of presentation arise from the social balance between individual and community,

24. States, *Great Reckonings in Little Rooms*, 3.

25. *Hegel on Tragedy* (ed. Anne and Henry Paolucci; New York: Harper & Row, 1975), 312; quoted in States, *Great Reckonings in Little Rooms*, 3.

> with the individual endowed with an appearance that heightens his superhuman qualities. Whatever passions or circumstances these schemes signify, the schemes themselves embody forces other than the fictive or mimetic. What we find among the Greeks is similar to what we find at the initial stages of any dramatic tradition and what we are finding in the developments of the twentieth century. . . . Whether the form that did arise came about purely because of socio-religious influence or was partly the result of esthetic play, may be impossible to ever discover. But whatever its genesis, an act-scheme [mode of presentation] embodies in its structure a resolution or impulses stemming from deep social causes. As presentation, these act-schemes not only provide a form for displaying these varied impulses but also serve as a means of transcending the limits that contain them.[26]

The scribe, as both creator and presenter of prophetic texts, takes control over both the scheme, or mode of presentation, and the content. The prophet's power, though given to him by the Lord, could only be enacted by the prophet himself until the scribe appropriated the character of the prophet. In reality, scribes had the governing structures of prophetic performance before them for a long period of time, providing them with a range of language, gesture, and activity to which they could bring shape and form. However, to do this, the scribe had to wrest the performative away from the prophet and put in on the page.

Scribe as Performer

If the scribe effectively diminished and replaced the social power of the charismatic prophetic performer, that does not mean that the scribe was not a performer as well. In fact, a second level of performative investigation needs to be applied to the prophetic texts. Not only was there an original oral performance by the prophet, but there was a "re-performance" that must be considered as the scribe transformed the oral performance to written text.

26. Beckerman, *Theatrical Presentation*, 104–5.

This representation is by no means a secondary or less important performance, as David Stacey explains: "When an oracle passes from the spoken to the written word, it gains in force and validity."[27]

This movement from oral to written is not a simple process between two poles of a dichotomy.[28] As did James Crenshaw, Michael Floyd explores the educational analogy for orality in texts and suggests that a complex interplay between written and oral existed,

> not only between education and literacy (even in the context of schooling) but also between audience and the readership of texts composed and transmitted in writing. . . . The author of such a text can thus aim to reach a relatively large audience through a relatively small readership because there are situations in which those able to read the text can mediate its contents to those who may be unable to do so.[29]

Certainly, the biblical texts provide evidence of the practice of public readings stretching all the way from Deuteronomy through Ezra and Nehemiah. Based upon his earlier observations, Floyd concludes that "documents were not necessarily written in order to reach a reading audience."[30] The implication is that the mode of thought more commonly associated with oral communication was used in the written communication. In much the same way that a TV news anchor "reads" the news script for the benefit of his listening audience, the scribes that produced (at least some of) the prophetic documents wrote to benefit those who had "ears to hear." Such scribal activity has been observed in a number of contexts. Robert Culley quotes the Anglo-Saxon scholar A. N. Doane who writes, "The scribe-as-performer would see the rewriting as enhancing the traditional text by giving it life in the present, by making it 'more real.'"[31] The scribe of the prophetic perform-

27. David Stacey, *Prophetic Drama in the Old Testament* (London: Epworth, 1990), 232.

28. Michael Floyd has provided a helpful summary of a complex process in "'Write the Revelation!' (Hab 2:2): Re-imagining the Cultural History of Prophecy," in Ben Zvi and Floyd, *Writings and Speech in Israelite and Ancient Near Eastern Prophecy*, 103–43.

29. Ibid., 137.

30. Ibid., 139.

31. A. N. Doane, "The Ethnography of Scribal Writing and Anglo-Saxon Poetry: Scribe as Performer," *Oral Tradition* 9 (1994): 434; quoted in Robert Culley, "Orality and Writtenness in the Prophetic Texts," in Ben Zvi and Floyd, *Writings and Speech in Israelite and Ancient Near Eastern Prophecy*, 53.

ance enhanced the original performance by ordering, editing, and formalizing the prophetic utterance, thereby giving it "life in the present."

This scribe, much like the playwright, operated at the boundary between the oral and the written. That boundary place is the same occupied by the playwright who uses a written text to produce an oral performance; however, the prophetic scribe worked in the opposite direction. The playwright goes from text to performance, while the prophetic scribe used an oral performance to produce a written text. Raymond Person expressed the thought in this fashion, "As members of a primarily oral society, they [the scribes] undertook even their literate activity—that is, the copying of texts—with an oral mind-set."[32] As States explains, the playwright himself becomes the actor in the act of writing. He works out a character's possibilities "on the instrument of his own organism. . . . Composing for the actor, whether for the actor within oneself or the actor in one's theatre company, means simply composing for the human instrument with all its stops and ventages."[33] Yet a change took place. Horowitz and Samuels, linguists by trade, make the following important observation: "It is impossible to fathom the shift in mind (and soul) that emerged with the use of script and later the invention of print."[34]

Evidence for this oral mind-set or even the performative mode of thought comes from a variety of different sources. Person supports his case for an "oral mentality" through the examination of the Hebrew דבר. He suggests that this word signifies a concept that may, and in fact does, include more than the single grammatical unit signified by the English "word" and understood within the context of a literate society. The Hebrew דבר is not a literary notion but is an idea that may be better understood as "'utterance,' 'speech,' or 'message.'"[35] Since the same utterance or message can be conveyed in a number of ways, that which has been labeled by text critics as "alternative readings or variants" of the primary text may in fact be evidence of the oral mind-set of the scribe that considers these as synonymous renditions of the same oral proclamation.

32. Raymond Person, "The Ancient Israelite Scribe as Performer," *Journal of Biblical Literature* 117 (1998): 602.

33. States, *Great Reckonings in Little Rooms*, 131–32.

34. Rosalind Horowitz and S. Jay Samuels, "Comprehending Oral and Written Language: Critical Contrasts for Literacy and Schooling," in *Comprehending Oral and Written Language* (ed. Rosalind Horowitz and S. Jay Samuels; New York: Academic Press, 1987), 18.

Perhaps an appeal to an analogy drawn from the theatre may be useful. The playwright composes the script fully aware that each rendition or performance of the script will contain variation not only of the text spoken but of emphasis, diction, and posture, making each performance of the play unique. This unique "re-presenting" is resident in the Hebrew דבר, particularly as the prophetic word is presented as "Thus says the Lord." As States describes this relationship in the theatre, it is the actor's awareness that he is the theatre's only conduit:

> He is the original of the poet's "copy" in the sense that he is the being who grants it an existence. The poet may have conceived the words, but insofar as they are true they are borrowed from nature; they are what he heard as his imagination listened to the world. To this degree, all dramatic texts are hypotheses, yearnings. The poet records his vision of the world as an imitation of a possible truth. And behold, the actor appears and validates his vision, as nature validates the vision of the physicist by behaving naturally. The actor is living proof that the play is true: he takes the words from the poet's lips and gives them back. . . . In other words, the poet's copy falls into nature in the form of a demonstration. One might say that becoming Hamlet or Juliet the actor throws himself into the gap between the hypothetical and the real.[36]

This is precisely the "gap" the scribe sought to inhabit: that space between the prophet as person (Amos the shepherd from Tekoa) and the prophet as character (Amos the deliverer of oracles and visions).

PERFORMATIVE MODE OF THOUGHT IN A TEXT

How then can we identify a performative mode of thought within a given text? Must we be content with identifying speech forms that have been taken over either in whole or part by a composer of texts? Or can we find a deep structure that unfolds itself in performance criticism?

---

35. Person, "Ancient Israelite Scribe as Performer," 604.

36. States, *Great Reckonings in Little Rooms*, 126–27.

In developing a taxonomy by which to examine written texts for listening audiences, we turn once again to insights provided in the field of linguistics. Oesterreicher has attempted a "description of the underlying communicative constellations that control the production of such texts or text groups of the type labeled orality in text."[37] He defines the following categories:

1. Writing by semiliterate persons: "The texts written by these semiliterate individuals—or the texts dictated by them in the case they are unable to write personally—generally display linguistic elements and procedures that are, as a rule, alien to written communication: on the one hand, they show us the universal characteristics of the language of immediacy, for instance, anacoluthons, repetitions, and vagueness of referentialization or inconsistencies in deictic orientation; on the other hand, in these texts we find grammatical and lexical features of diatopic, diastratic, and diaphasic varieties that generally violate the norms of written communication."[38]
2. Writing by bilingual persons in diglossic situation: "In those instances in which writers are not acquainted with the high variety of the dominant language, they tend to use non-exemplary varieties that are the only means available for them to express themselves linguistically."
3. Relaxed writing: "Persons who are well trained and thus perfectly able to conform to all linguistic and textual norms need not, in all circumstances, write according to the prescriptions of written style. . . . This style is most likely to occur in strictly private texts, for instance, personal notes and records or letters to close friends."
4. Records of spoken transaction: "As we have seen, medial transcoding makes it possible to represent phonic utterance of any type in script." Oesterreicher observes that it is the particular circumstance of the locution that determines the linguistic immediacy in the transcribed text. In this category of communicative constellations the notion of performative mode of thought has special applicability.
5. Writing adjusted to lower competence of readers: "Here, a writer who

37. Wulf Oesterreicher, "Types of Orality in Text," in *Written Voices, Spoken Signs,* (ed. Egbert Bakker and Ahuvia Kahane; Cambridge, Mass.: Harvard University Press, 1997), 200.

38. The quotations in this list are from Oesterreicher, "Types of Orality in Text," 201–5.

possesses the high competence and skill needed to formulate a precise and elaborate linguistic style is opting for expressions of the immediacy type for the sake of easier comprehension by the reader or in order to create a certain intimacy."

6. Writing subjected to "simple" discourse traditions or genres: "In this case, orality in text refers to communicative strategies that result from a strict orientation at conceptual simplicity of language and composition." That is, the text type chosen by the author determines the degree of orality in the text. For example, a novelist can with understandable clarity include dialogue within the novel as the characters of the story play out the action.
7. Writing according to plain-style rhetoric: "It is characteristic of this style to draw on a number of features that have been conventionalized in a certain literary tradition in order to create the impression of naturalness, spontaneity, simplicity, and ease." It is not an imitation of the language of immediacy but an attempt to achieve the effect of oral immediacy in the written text. This technique can be observed in editorial comments inserted into a text that give the impression of an inserted whisper from the writer to the reader in order to explain some part of the surrounding text.
8. Mimesis of immediacy or simulated orality: This type of orality in text is an imitation of the oral immediacy. "As opposed to the 'plain style' imperative that does not aim at imitation of concrete oral utterances but aspires to the linguistic expression of naturalness and simplicity, simulated orality incorporates linguistic material that is taken over directly from the language of immediacy."

In reflecting on the above eight types of textual immediacy, Oesterreicher suggests that the "phenomena of orality in poetic or literary texts . . . must be examined with caution because they normally do not reflect spontaneous or natural language but functionalize select features of linguistic immediacy."[39] The contention that we are making in this chapter is that one of the "select features of linguistic immediacy" that has become functionalized in

39. Ibid., 206.

portions of the Hebrew prophets is a performative mode of thought.

Martti Nissinen suggests that Near Eastern prophecy was an oral performance that was retransmitted both orally and in written form. The written form was used to communicate to an audience distant from the speaker, both geographically and chronologically, and to assist in the recall of the original prophetic communication.[40] Nissinen concludes that the scribal process of writing an oracle for the benefit of a new listening audience is an important part of the prophetic process:

> The intermediaries, addressees, and interpreters of the prophetic messages, hence are not mere instruments and objects of the divine word, but active participants whose needs and preferences keep the process advancing. Without their participation, there is no meaningful message to be heard and heeded, no communication, no prophecy.[41]

In other words, no scribe—no prophecy. Yet the commitment of the oral performance to writing changed the dynamics of the communication event. For one, the relationship between the communication and the communicator changed. E. A. Havelock makes the following observation: "In orality the speaker and his speech remained one, what was spoken was his creation, in a sense it was himself."[42] The transference to a written medium unraveled that close connection between speaker and speech. In a written medium, language assumed a new identity. "As language assumed a new identity," Havelock continues, "so did the personality that spoke and used it."[43]

This transcendence of person brings us close to the concepts applied to performance criticism. "A good presentational idea," writes Beckerman, "juxtaposes performer and audience or performer and performer in circumstances that exploit the maximum potential for attention, excitement and deep response."[44] In performative terms, we experience "an event in which a

---

40. Martti Nissinen, "Spoken, Written, Quoted, and Invented: Orality and Writtenness in Ancient Near Eastern Prophecy," in Ben Zvi and Floyd, *Writings and Speech in Israelite and Ancient Near Eastern Prophecy*, 268.

41. Ibid., 270–71.

42. E. A. Havelock, "The Coming of Literate Communication to Western Civilization," *Journal of Communication* 30 (1980): 98.

43. Ibid.

44. Beckerman, *Theatrical Presentation*, 11.

mortal human being, someone like ourselves, appears to exceed mortal boundaries, and—this is most important—he takes us with him beyond those boundaries."[45] It is in performance that the dialectic of the human and the super-human—or the human and the divine, in the case of the prophets—is found. The performers (prophet and scribe) "set into motion a vibration between actual presence and the idea which informs the performance."[46] This projection of energy is the "field of force" that binds the performers and spectators to the act performed. "When it is spontaneous and vigorous, it stimulates the sensation of transcendency."[47]

In some ways, the journey from prophetic pronouncement to written text is parallel to the journey from orality to text taken by the epic poems Oesterreicher has analyzed. Oesterreicher contends that the process begins with a face-to-face communication that he labels a "communication-in-performance."[48] This communication-in-performance, although face-to-face, differs from everyday conversation in that the performer is not speaking as an individual to an individual but is addressing a group as a persona other than his own. Typically, this is more characteristic of distant communication, but the communicative profile of oral performance does not fully conform to the distinguishing marks of more distant communication. The performance, like distant communication, is generally monologic and reflective, lacking the spontaneity and dialogue typical of immediate orality. Unlike distant communication, however, it must state explicitly all relevant information; the performer can operate through immediate communication by the use of paralinguistic features such as body posture, tone, pause, facial expression, gestures, and staging that can be used to assist the oral communication.[49]

Oesterreicher uses an additional set of concepts in discussing textual orality. Borrowing from the work of Heinrich Lausberg, Oesterreicher considers the distinction between a "self-consuming discourse" and a "reusable discourse."[50] The language of immediacy belongs to the first

45. Ibid., 21.

46. Ibid., 22.

47. Ibid.

48. Oesterreicher, "Types of Orality in Text," 207.

49. Ibid., 209.

50. Ibid., 211. See Heinrich Lausberg, *Romanische Sprachwissenschaft* (vol. 1; Berlin: De Gruyter, 1969).

category. This type of discourse is spontaneous and dependent upon the personal interaction between participants at that time and that place. The language of distance, however, is reusable discourse that is conditioned by traditional themes and formulations. Successful epic performers, much like the Hebrew prophets, were skilled because of their proficiency at *mouvance*, the ability to adjust the performance to the immediate audience. That is, the successful prophet, in the act of speaking, would take a traditional and reusable discourse and make it appear immediate and self-consuming. The scribe would do just the reverse by making the self-consuming performance of the prophet reusable in a text. Epics and prophetic texts will "never show the same degree of definiteness and reification that is characteristic of written or literate texts" because the prophetic text also includes, embedded in it, an orality, that is, an element of the performer's *mouvance*.[51] "The *mouvance* of the epic discourse represents a mitigation of extreme distance, although it must never be identified with the provisionality of immediacy in colloquial or informal speech."[52] Oesterreicher contends that, at least for epic, the features that resemble orality are not intended to imitate orality but function differently from the linguistic and discourse material that pertains to casual conversation.[53]

Oesterreicher concludes, "The presentation of the already known of tradition and group identity is further enhanced by the staged epic discourse and the strategies of highlighting the moment of the *we-now-here* in the performative act."[54] That is, the impression of linguistic immediacy created by epic performance that reinforces the identity of the *we* (association between speakers) in the *here* and *now* (shared context) creates openness to the communicative intent of the writer/speaker. The use of the oral style in a written text is a "very effective device to influence people by creating the impression of traditionality and authenticity."[55] Oesterreicher concludes, in his consideration of epic, "Epic performance thus proves itself a vital means for the social construction of reality and for controlling social dynamics."[56]

---

51. Oesterreicher, "Types of Orality in Text," 211.
52. Ibid.
53. Ibid., 213.
54. Ibid.
55. Ibid.
56. Ibid.

ORALITY IN TEXT: SOCIAL POWER

We suggest the same holds true for the Hebrew prophets and that the orality in text is an important strategy for the use of social power. Oesterreicher suggests that epic poems—and we would include the prophetic documents—were written "not only for the preservation of tradition but also with a deliberate intent to modify or even manipulate existing traditions for new purposes."[57] In this dialectic between performers and spectators that Beckerman labels "dialectic presentation," a key feature is the fact that those involved do not have total control over what is happening.[58] In iconic modes of performance (e.g., parades, shows of glorification) space supersedes time because the spatial unfolding of the event is the dominant factor. In dialectic modes of performance, time supersedes the spatial, because "we watch the performer move toward the critical points of the act, figuratively or literally holding our breath."[59] As spectators, we do this in the here and now. The time of the dialectical exchange is the eternal present—the effect of immediacy, in Oesterreicher's terms, or of giving the prophetic tradition "life in the present," according to A. Doane. In fact, oral immediacy and physical immediacy are two of the distinctive features of theatrical and dramatic performance. As Beckerman suggests, "Theatre occurs when another or others, isolated in time space, present themselves to another or others."[60] By imitating conceptional orality or linguistic immediacy, the prophetic documents create, in Oesterreicher's words, "an atmosphere of confidence and solidarity."[61]

Performance combines a system of presentation with narrative materials derived from and influenced by the sensibilities of the creators. For example, Greek tragedy's alternating sequence of odes and episodes provided the tragedians with a system for communicating extended narrative material in which the choral odes sought to bring the events of the episodes into harmony with some larger vision of the events and to compress time into a highly concentrated experience for the spectators. In *Oedipus the King*, for

57. Ibid., 214.

58. Beckerman, *Theatrical Presentation*, 56.

59. Ibid.

60. Bernard Beckerman, *Dynamics of Drama: Theory and Method of Analysis* (New York: Drama Book Specialists, 1979), 9.

61. Oesterreicher, "Types of Orality in Text," 214.

example, the five major episodes of action separated by choral odes presents us with no more than a day in the lives of the play's characters, yet the whole life story of Oedipus and his beloved Thebes is also present. The play opens with a chorus of suppliants come to beg Oedipus to do something to lift the plague from Thebes. Oedipus replies, "I sent Creon, my wife's own brother, to Delphi—Apollo the Prophet's oracle—to learn what I might do or say to save our city. *Today's the day. When I count days gone by it torments me.*"[62] The past and the present, and by implication the future, are brought together in the here and now. The story of Thebes and the life of Oedipus are compressed into the plot structure and conventions that came to dominate Athenian tragedy both in its literary manifestation and in its performance structures. Each episode brings us closer to the play's ultimate crux: Oedipus's discovery that he murdered his father and married his mother. The overall schematic of the play moves by compressing past, present, and future into an inescapable moment of self-confrontation (*we-now-here*). The similarities to the episodic structure of *Oedipus the King* and Amos's oracles against foreign nations are striking. This is not to imply that they have parallel literary structures, but that the action of the episodes of *Oedipus* and the action of the oracles of Amos have similar performance structures.[63] Though we will deal specifically with the oracles of Amos in a later chapter, a brief comparison of the active structures of *Oedipus* and the oracles will help establish a clearer framework.

Oedipus the King

Prologue: Oedipus confronts the suppliants at his palace gate to find out what they want from him. Creon arrives from the Oracle at Delphi with a command to punish the murderer of Laius (who resides in Thebes) in order to lift the plague from Thebes. Despite Creon's desire to share the news privately, Oedipus insists on public disclosure of the oracle. Oedipus swears to find and punish the murderer.

62. Sophocles, *Oedipus the King*, in *The Three Theban Plays* (trans. Robert Fagles; New York: Penguin, 1982), 162 (italics ours).

63. Action is the result of performers pursuing the projects of characters. This concept is more fully developed in chapter 3. However, it is essential at this point to remember that our definition of action is a performance definition.

Choral Ode: The chorus, not knowing Creon's news, chants to the gods for mercy on Thebes.

Episode: Oedipus declares his curse on the murderer of Laius and his intent to find and punish him with banishment. Tiresias, the blind prophet, warns Oedipus that he is the curse and the murderer he seeks. Oedipus accuses Creon of a conspiracy. Tiresias leaves with one final warning to Oedipus that he will discover himself as the murderer.

Choral Ode: The chorus tries to reconcile what it has heard. It acknowledges Zeus and Apollo as knowing the truth and resolves to wait for proof of Oedipus's guilt.

Episode: Oedipus confronts Creon and refuses to accept the charges against him. Oedipus and Creon debate the truth and trade accusations against each other. Jocasta, the queen, Oedipus's mother and wife, reveals the story of the oracle against Laius and how the baby spoken of was bound by the ankles and flung onto a mountainside. Oedipus's growing recognition that he is indeed the guilty one forces him to reveal his own story. He demands that the servant who survived Laius's death be brought before him. Only this man can determine Oedipus's innocence or guilt.

Choral Ode: The chorus chants of the relationship between gods and man, of destiny and of laws from on high. The action of the play is about to be fulfilled, and the truth (particularly for the Athenian spectator of this play) rests on the fulfillment of the prophecies as a confirmation of the powers of heaven:

> Pride breeds the tyrant
> violent pride, gorging, crammed to bursting
> with all that is overripe and rich with ruin—
> clawing up to the heights, headlong pride
> crashes down the abyss—sheer doom!
> No footing helps, all foothold lost and gone.
> But the healthy strife that makes the city strong—
> I pray that god will never end that wrestling:
> god, my champion, I will never let you go.
>
> But if any man comes striding, high and mighty
> in all he says and does,

no fear of justice, no reverence
for the temples of the gods—
let a rough doom tear him down,
repay his pride, breakneck, ruinous pride!
If he cannot reap his profits fairly
cannot restrain himself from outrage—
mad, laying hands on the holy things untouchable!

Can such a man, so desperate, still boast
he can save his life from the flashing bolts of god?
If all such violence goes with honor now
why join the sacred dance?[64]

Episode: A messenger arrives with news of the death of the king of Corinth, the man who raised Oedipus as his own. The messenger reveals that it was he who found Oedipus on the mountainside and delivered him to the king and queen of Corinth. Oedipus's moment of recognition is at hand. Oedipus demands that the old shepherd who was charged with throwing the baby away on the mountainside be brought forward. Jocasta begs Oedipus not to do so and pronounces his doom. Oedipus declares, "Let it burst! Whatever will, whatever must!"[65]

Choral Ode: The chorus dances and chants its praise of Apollo.

Episode: The shepherd arrives. The messenger confronts him with the truth. Oedipus threatens the shepherd with death if he does not reveal what he knows. The shepherd reveals Oedipus's true identity. The remaining action of the play represents a *decrescence,* or movement away from the primary conflict, ending with an *exodus,* a conventionalized ending of Athenian tragedy.[66]

From a performance point of view, the episodes of *Oedipus* are built on specific human behaviors and interactions (debates, confrontation, propitiation) that allow the playwright to deal with expansive material in a highly

64. Sophocles, *Oedipus the King* (trans. Fagles), 209–10.

65. Ibid., 224.

66. We deal more fully with decrescence in chapter 3, as part of our analysis of the text of Amos.

compressed fashion. The debates over truth, justice, and the authority of the oracles created the opportunity for the larger story of Oedipus and of Thebes to come into play. Much of this material was from an oral tradition and a performance tradition that existed at least eighty years before Sophocles. By the time the traditional scheme of tragedy emerged, it was already a fixed system of debates, verbal confrontations, and lamentations. The key performative features evident in our brief description of Oedipus's action are as follows:

- The play contains a compressed plot/story ratio. What happens in the episodes happens in less than a day but incorporates a story that takes place over years. For the actor, this is highly significant. Figuring out how to play Oedipus as he moves from moment to moment in a single day of his life is an entirely different problem than playing Oedipus across the span of his life. (A playwright could easily reverse this ratio, thereby creating an entirely different play.)
- Both the odes and episodes are structured according to specific human activity (e.g., debating, chanting/praying, confronting, accusing, denying). Even the famous messenger speech, in which the spectators learn of Jocasta's suicide and Oedipus's blinding, is a mode of reporting that was part of the traditional scheme of tragedy.
- The movement between odes and episodes, or from more distant modes of communication to the immediacy of the episodes, facilitates the rising and falling action. The actor playing Oedipus relies on the choral odes to help manipulate the transitions from episode to episode, and uses the dynamics of the odes as part of his relationship with the spectators. (On a more practical level, this also provides actors with an opportunity to change masks and prepare for new episodes.)

If we look at an overview of the performed action of Amos's oracles against the foreign nations, we see a pattern of action that resonates strongly with the pattern evident in *Oedipus*. It is not the literary pattern we are comparing, but the performative pattern (space-time-activity). As a performance term, action results from doing, whether one is an actor, a storyteller, a scribe reading the text to a live audience, or Amos himself, prophesying to the people of Israel.

Oracles against Foreign Nations

Amos's delivering of the oracles against foreign nations is a highly compressed event with very clear space-time implications. He is addressing people of the northern kingdom who have gathered, or have been gathered, around him. The entire event may only take a total of ten to fifteen minutes, culminating in the oracle against Israel, but the larger story of God's relationship to Israel emerges as Amos moves from territory to territory. The performance time of the oracles is the time of here and now. Amos moves quickly through a pattern of identifying the transgressions (accusation), stating the punishment (threat), and delivering the result. A pattern of movement is established with the repeated "Thus says the LORD . . . says the LORD" declarations. This pattern, though not the same as the choral ode pattern in literary terms, has essentially the same performance function: helping to establish variety and intensity, distance and proximity. This pattern also facilitates Amos's moves between prophet and voice of God.[67]

Damascus → Gaza → Tyre → Edom → Ammonites → Moab → Judah → Israel

Amos moves the spectators to a moment of recognition for the people of Israel. Like *Oedipus,* this is a drama in which the moment of recognition is accompanied by a reversal of fortune, for the people of Israel will suffer the following:

So, I will press you down in your place,
  just as a cart presses down
  when it is full of sheaves.
Flight shall perish from the swift,
  and the strong shall not retain their strength,
  nor shall the mighty save their lives;
those who handle the bow shall not stand,
  and those who are swift of foot shall not save themselves,

67. These ideas are more fully developed in chapter 4 but are also essential to the prophet-scribal relationship, as our understanding of Amos the prophet is largely mediated by the scribe's text.

nor shall those who ride horses save their lives;
and those who are stout of heart among the mighty
shall flee away naked in that day,
says the LORD. (Amos 2:13–16)

Just as each episode of *Oedipus* moves both characters and spectators closer to the resolution of the drama, so each oracle moves Amos and his spectators in the same direction. The *action* is the result of specific human activity occurring simultaneously in the time of the drama and the reality of the lives of the spectators. In the case of both Sophocles and Amos, the pattern of action that we have is the result of a writer. However, in both cases, the writers (playwright and scribe) have appropriated a performance tradition that preceded them. In the case of the scribe, that tradition includes both the reality of Amos's life as prophet and the oral tradition that followed.

ORALITY IN TEXT: PERFORMATIVE MODE OF THOUGHT

In the first chapter, we proposed the model of a "variable discourse grid." We can now place discursive characteristics on that grid as a means of locating pertinent characteristics of a performative mode of thought in a given piece of literature. The vertical axis represents a linguistic *conceptual mode* of discourse that moves from the immediate to the distant forms of discourse. The horizontal axis represents a linguistic *medium* of discourse moving from the oral to the written form of discourse.

VARIABLE DISCOURSE GRID

Immediate
Linguistic Conceptional Mode

Conversation Mode
Face-to-face
Uses nonlinguistic cues
Primary discourse is interpersonal
Structureless, simple linear
Action oriented, narrative-like
Event oriented, spontaneous
Story oriented, self-consuming
Fleeting, vague
Repetitive in given space-time
Informal, here and now
Cohesion expressed through reference to items outside the discourse

Performative Mode
Suspends real space-time
Creates virtual space-time
Creates imaginative space-time
Experiential
Traditional
Reusable
Relaxed

Oral ← → Written
(Linguistic medium) (Linguistic medium)

Lecture Mode

Creates cognitive space-time
Segmented space-time
Reflective
Monologic
Idea oriented
Fleeting

Text Mode

Multiple predication
Face-to-text
Permanent
Formal
Future and past
Not space-time bound
Explicitness in text (references other parts of text)
Idea oriented
Argument oriented
Explanatory prose

Distant
Linguistic Conceptional Mode

The graph should not be taken to imply that choices are made between one quadrant or another, but rather the graph is a way to represent the dominance of one set of characteristics over another within a text. A given piece of literature may reside to the far corner of one quadrant due to the dominance of one set of linguistic characteristics over another, or it may be plotted near the axis of the lines because of shared linguistic characteristics. That is, the author-performer's mouvance must be considered in forming a description of discourse resident in a given piece of literature.

CHAPTER THREE

Prophets and Performance

Although the book of Amos contains perhaps the best example of the performance mode of thought, other prophetic books provide clear examples of this idea. First Samuel, for example, offers a clear instance of the tension between presentation and telling. The relative familiarity with the narrative and plot of I Samuel makes an easier transition to performance criticism for those of us not accustomed to using performance criticism terminology. There already exists some literature in biblical studies that has begun making application of theatre to the literature of I Samuel, and it will serve us well to begin with that literature and build on it. Even though the bulk of the second half of this book focuses on one of the minor prophets, our contention is that this "performative mode of thought" in the Israelite intellectual economy was applied much more broadly than simply to the books of the later prophets. The use of I Samuel in this chapter serves as a reminder of that broad application.

I SAMUEL 3

In *The Bible as Theatre,* Shimon Levy argues that I Sam 3 contains many characteristics common to theatre and ritual.[1] The chapter is given to that

1. Shimon Levy, *The Bible as Theatre* (Portland: Sussex Academic Press, 2002), 15.

wonderful interchange between the Lord, Samuel, and Eli. The bulk of the chapter is played out during the stillness of night, which is interrupted by the intrusion of the demanding presence of the Lord. The Lord interrupts Samuel's sleep, and Samuel in turn interrupts the sleep of Eli. Not until the third interruption does Eli finally realize the true nature of these divine disturbances, but even he cannot foresee the true extent of the changes in store for both himself and his young apprentice.

The characteristics of theatre and ritual, writes Levy, "constitute the basis of the dialogical situation, which mediates between the Here and the Beyond, between the then and the now."[2] By seeing this passage of Samuel as potential theatre, Levy argues that certain qualities can be uncovered that might be missed by a strictly literary analysis, and that the passage constitutes a "scene" that occurred and can be reconstructed as "theatre." The primary quality Levy isolates is a belief that language creates reality in addition to just describing it:

> [First Samuel 3] clearly reveals a belief in the creative word, a conviction that language not only describes reality but also creates it. This quality of language constitutes a link between theatre, whether secular or religious, and the Bible, both of which understand language as action. The first ten verses describe the initiation ritual by which the boy Samuel becomes a prophet.[3]

In addition to a linguistic study of the biblical text, Levy applies an analysis of the passage using the language of theatrical analysis: time, space, props, set design, lighting, and movement. In fact, Levy's analysis moves fluidly between literary, dramatic, and performance analysis, with particular emphasis on the linguistic function of the text. Most importantly, Levy identifies Samuel not as an "artistic fictitious drama that recreates extra-theatrical reality for the sake of entertainment, but rather a multi-sensual presentation of trans-sensual events that operates on many levels of consciousness and is described by means of theatrical tools."[4] In the story in I Sam 3 we have the possibility of several different kinds of events: the prophetic act itself (having occurred at some point in history), the oral tradition of that prophetic

2. Ibid.
3. Ibid.
4. Ibid., 37.

event, the scribal event that codified the oral tradition, and the reading and rereading of the prophetic text by scribes and others to a gathered audience. Together, all of these events create a formidable performance history for prophetic literature. By necessity, investigations of this history focus primarily on the biblical text. The method of analysis we propose also focuses on the biblical text, or as we will refer to it, the script. What we are proposing has a number of things in common with the work of Levy, as well as that of David Stacey and others, particularly as we make use of theatrical tools for describing and thinking about what is presented to us in the prophetic text. However, in our exploration of the relationship between scribe, prophet, text, and audience, we extend beyond most examples of current theatrical analysis by integrating the function and impact of theatre and performance as part of that analysis.

Levy's method of theatrical analysis is essentially a horizontal method that functions by striation. As Beckerman writes, in the conventionalized horizontal method of analysis "plot is analyzed as a vein running through a play; character and spectacle are other veins; theme, above all, is disentangled from the rest and examined separately. . . . The habit of mind that chooses to treat a play as a collection of strands inhibits an appreciation of it as a sequence of total experiences."[5] Theatre, and more specifically the drama, is not a thing but an event, an experience meant to be shared between presenters and spectators. As such, theatrical and dramatic events are more than the sum of their parts. It is not so much our ability to identify the parts that matters, but our ability to understand how the parts function together to create the event. Having the event itself to analyze is ideal, as in the case of a Broadway play, a ballet, or the prophetic act itself. In the absence of the event itself, we turn to the written text, along with other evidence available to us, to "reconstruct" the drama. As Levy's work demonstrates, when we use theatrical tools, we engage in a process that parallels that of the theatre artist. But by simply describing the biblical text as theatre through the use of theatrical tools, what is accomplished is really only part of the process: the identification and explanation of formal elements (plot, props, setting). These are indeed constituent elements of theatre, but until we put them back together, or see how they

5. Bernard Beckerman, *Dynamics of Drama: Theory and Method of Analysis* (New York: Drama Book Specialists, 1979), 36.

work together to create the event, we have not fully explored the potential drama embedded in the biblical text. It is our understanding of the event and the potential impact of that experience that really leads us to a discovery of the power of the scribe, a power that originally belonged to the prophet. Put simply, it is our ability to imagine the drama, to experience it as an event, by operating in a performance mode of thought, that leads us directly to the scribe-prophet relationship and the power of the prophetic text.

We are not simply describing events from prophetic literature by means of theatrical tools, but investigating prophetic actions and oracles as part of the larger complex of Hebrew thought.

THEATRE AND DRAMA DEFINED

> Theatre occurs when one or more human beings, isolated in time and/or space, present themselves to another or others.
>
> Drama occurs when one or more human beings, isolated in time and/or space, present themselves in imagined acts to another or others.
> Bernard Beckerman, *Dynamics of Drama*

Theatre and drama are organically connected under the umbrella of *presentation*. The breadth of the working definitions Beckerman provides allows us to go beyond specific forms of theatre and drama that are expressions of cultural and historical periods such as Greek or Elizabethan tragedy, realism, or naturalism. The definitions represent a theory of theatre and drama as specific media of presentation regardless of historical forms. In fact, as Eli Rozik points out, theatre is ahistorical when understood as a method of presentation or representation:

> Methods of representation, including theatre, can be and are used for doing things; but they have no intrinsic intentions or purposes. Only the action of which they are a part can be said to have purposes and effects. Even if ritual employs a theatrical text as part of its practice, and subordinates it to its particular aim, the medium itself cannot originate from such a particular use of it. The use of the medium of theatre logically presupposes its existence. By nature rituals are

> historical: they are established and disappear; theatre, in contrast, is a-historical: as a medium it exists even if it is not used.[6]

It is in this context that we view the prophetic tradition. Thus, theatrical presentation offers the framework for understanding prophetic tradition. Though there may be material limits to our knowledge of what the prophets did before the literary tradition created by the scribes, we know that tradition existed and it was a tradition of presentation. The oracles, visions, and actions inscribed by the literary tradition point to a tradition of presentation, and therefore of performance, that readily lends itself to the type of performance criticism we are proposing. Consider the interplay between the oral and the written in the following quotation from Ehud Ben Zvi:

> Oral communication reigned in the society in which the literati lived. This being the case, if they were to serve as brokers of divine knowledge to the vast majority of the population, the literati must have read to the general population and interpreted for them pieces of prophetic literature. . . . In other words, a written text becomes the starting point for oral presentation. Needless to say, the communicative event here involves not only the written text or a portion thereof, but also how it is read or proclaimed and the interaction between audience and speaker. Under these social conditions, it is reasonable to assume that an authoritative written text becomes the starting point for the oral performances of the literati and the aurality of an audience.[7]

Ben Zvi goes on to write:

> It is probable and even likely that the literati were also trained for skillful speech. If so, who, where, and by whom were they trained to be good communicators/orators/read-

6. Eli Rozik, *The Ritual Roots of Theatre: Rethinking Ritual and Other Theories of Origin* (Iowa City: University of Iowa Press, 2002), 27–28.

7. Ehud Ben Zvi, "Introduction: Writings, Speeches, and the Prophetic Books—Setting an Agenda" in *Writings and Speech in Israelite and Ancient Near Eastern Prophecy* (ed. Ehud Ben Zvi and Michael H. Floyd; Atlanta: Society of Biblical Literature, 2000), 16.

> ers? All things considered, it seems likely that these scribal brokers of YHWH's word communicated to society as a whole a set of related oral "texts," each informing the others, within the general discourse of the period.[8]

What Ben Zvi describes here bears a striking resemblance to the process by which a performance tradition is formed. Particularly since what Ben Zvi suggests is predicated upon the "scribal brokers" negotiating a relationship between existing "oral texts" (performances) and the creation of written texts (scripts). As Beckerman writes:

> Every age seems to find certain recurrent activities peculiarly satisfying. Through the interaction of performers and spectators over a period of time, it amasses a representative collection of activities from which later writers and performers can choose and to which the most original of them contributes. . . . In drama each individual creative choice is made within a frame of socio-aesthetic practice so that the theatre artist naturally selects his materials from a context of expectation.[9]

THE SOCIAL SET OF CONSTRUCTED ACTIVITY

Examples of this "context of expectation" exist for every period of theatre history: the Greeks and debate, Shakespeare and trials, Shakespeare and weddings, mistaken identity and deception in the commedia dell'arte tradition, and so on. The products of a presentational or performative tradition (patterns of dramatic activity) refer spectators not to personal experience but to the socioaesthetic conventions they represent. In performance, the activity of the performer points to these socioaesthetic conventions. In Beckerman's terms, the activity represents an *imagined act*, which is drawn from the socioaesthetic conventions that are established in any given historical period. In prophetic terms, *delivering an oracle* is part of the *act* of prophesying. This in no way should suggest that what the prophets did was false, in the colloquial

8. Ibid., 17.

9. Beckerman, *Dynamics of Drama*, 23.

sense of "putting on an act." The act is nothing more than the structure of organization the performer must have in order to communicate effectively to spectators. The act itself can contain both natural and artificial, or constructed, activity. In fact, as Beckerman points out, the history of theatre is filled with more examples of artificial than of natural activity: "Speaking in blank verse, expressing anger through the conventionalized stance of the Kabuki, and wearing masks are all varieties of behavior constructed for dramatic purpose."[10] In the context of presentation, constructed activity is no less "true" than natural activity; it is simply different.

Constructed dramatic activity, which is most often activity filtered through the imaginations of the creators of that activity, can be drawn from a variety of sources, including everyday activity. However, even the most naturalistic of dramatic activity reveals itself as separate and distinct from everyday reality. According to Ben Zvi, this was also the case with the post-monarchic prophetic literature. It is reasonable to assume that the efforts of the scribes to communicate through linguistic differentiation required, at least, an imaginative effort to know the communicative strategies of the prophets. The linguistic strategies of the text had to be differentiated from something, and that something is likely to have been an image of the prophet himself in performance.

> The post-monarchic scribes, who were responsible for the prophetic books in their present form, were careful to characterize the language of prophetic characters set in the monarchic period (with the exception of Jonah) in a distinctive manner. In these books, prophets speak a language that is most likely not identical to the language common in the province of Yehud in the Achaemenid period. If this is so, interesting matters of language (including lexical choices) and linguistic ideology emerge. The authors or redactors of these books are careful to communicate through linguistic differentiation that the words of YHWH associated with prophets from the late monarchic period did indeed sound different from everyday speech. This feature allows a text,

10. Ibid.

> composed or redacted in the not-so-distant-past, to convey a sense of distance from the present day, and also a sense of authority that comes from the ancient past. . . . This language distinction serves social needs.[11]

The goals Ben Zvi describes imply a manipulation of material for the text that would involve a process of selection and feedback, particularly if the language distinction served social needs. Both authors and redactors, by the process of reading and rereading, even if only for each other, would be engaged in a selection and feedback process that would shape the final form of the text. This is precisely how dramatic activity, from age to age, finds its way into the various structures that come to dominate theatrical practice. Dramatic activity is arranged into acts through a process of *selection* and *feedback* that is largely determined by interaction between performers and spectators, though other factors such as tradition, belief systems, and even law can affect the selection and feedback process. Ben Zvi describes a similar process when discussing prophetic literature and social formation:

> One of the most salient characteristics of the prophetic books is the frequent presence of multivalent words and expressions, generating additional and often multiple connotations, as well as puns and networks of intertextual associations informing one another. These features are expected and coherent in books that are to be read, reread, and studied generation after generation (cf. John 1:8; Hos. 14:10; Sir. 38:24–39:3). These features create a net of partial (re)readings of the text, informing and balancing each other. The different ways in which a particular unit within a prophetic book may be communicated orally—depending on the audience, the identity of the communicator, the social setting, and the particular occasion—are likely to inculcate in the memory of the wider community a network of received texts informing each other. . . .

11. Ben Zvi, "Introduction," 15.

> When a social group shares a particular collection of written works, the group memory shaped by these texts through the very act of reading and rereading them creates a sense of identity and continuity with the past; and the same holds true for the group's recollection of text-based speeches they have heard. . . .
>
> In addition, just as written texts can be taken out of their "original" context and brought into a new literary context, the same can be done orally through interpretation. In fact, high literacy and the expectation of continuous rereading led to the composition of written texts that not only furthered but also depended on the ability of readers and rereaders to "extract" literary elements out of their circumstances in the world of the text (e.g., prophetic or divine speeches associated with events in the monarchic period as construed by the text) and "appropriate" them. This process of recontextualization was necessary to allow the rereaders to identify with the (literary) Israel present within the world of the text. Significantly, a comparable but not identical process of recontextualization took place in oral retelling or ritual reading of a prophetic text or portions thereof, or, for that matter, in any oral telling of words and actions attributed to a prophet for the (monarchic) past in any social setting.[12]

Ben Zvi's identification of the key elements affecting the memory of a wider community—the particular unit within a prophetic book, the audience, the identity of the communicator, the social setting, and the occasion—are the precise elements necessary for theatre and drama to occur. The following chart compares elements common to discussions about the prophetic literature on the right with comparable concepts in theatre on the left.

12. Ibid., 18–19.

Actor/Presenter ⟷ Prophet/Scribe/Literati

Time Bound ⟷ Setting/Occasion

Space Bound ⟷ Setting/Occasion

Imagined Act ⟷ Unit of Prophetic Text

Audience/Spectators ⟷ Wider Community

DRAMA: SOMETHING THAT *OCCURS*

Theatre is wholly dependent upon human presence. "People make theatre occur. . . . They are consciously displaying themselves. . . . The performers manipulate the media for expressive purposes, while they themselves are the media being manipulated."[13] This does not mean that what occurs is always the fictional world of the drama. As Beckerman points out, to assume this is to ignore theatre's relationship to many other human activities, such as songs, dance, demonstrations, and lectures. And in all cases, the purpose of theatre is to affect spectators. In any conscious self-presentation there is the implication of someone to whom the presentation is being offered. In this sense, theatre, in its most primitive forms, is a gift. Theatre can contain, writes Beckerman, "anything man offers to others in his person."

> In primitive cultures there are instances where an entire social unit presents itself to the gods thus giving us the archetypal form of theatre. The spectator is a god or becomes god-endowed. Witnessing is an act of godhood though the temptation does arise in every age for the spectator to abandon his godhood and descend, whether to the dancing circle or to the stage, in order to participate in the presentation.[14]

13. Beckerman, *Dynamics of Drama*, 7.

14. Ibid., 8.

ISOLATED IN TIME AND SPACE

Isolation in time and space is the final element of our definition of theatre. For theatre to occur, performers and spectators must be separated from each other in order to establish the physical and psychological space for presentation and observance. The physical separation may be created by a circle, a wall, a raised platform, or any number of methods. The psychological space is manipulated by the performer, creating perceived distance and immediacy by a variety of skills and techniques. The manipulation of time, whether through the observation of sacred periods of presentation (e.g., rituals, holy days), or through devices that mark beginnings and endings such as, "Thus says the Lord," or "The Lord has spoken," reinforces the self-conscious nature of theatrical presentation. Beckerman explains: "Only through the knowledge and the power to conclude a showing do performers have the capacity to begin one. They divorce themselves from actual life and enter into imaginative existence. Without isolation and temporal control, presentation is merely life."[15]

Thus, theatre takes material and experience from life that can be turned into performance and does so through the act of presentation. Isolation and temporal control not only signify an act of self-conscious presentation but also the presence of the spectator; an exchange is taking place between at least two parties. In performance (what the performer does), an act of presentation (something offered to the public) occurs.

> [Presentation] is rooted in the idea of offering a gift, in particular offering a gift by making it present, of the moment. Presentation thus not only incorporates the act of giving, but also the act of being—of the donor being in touch with the receiver of the gift. To this temporal connotation is also tied a kinesthetic one, of presence, of the donor not only existing in the now of the receiver but also existing in that now as a vibrant individual. Hence, presentation alludes to a thing offered, a double-natured thing, a thing that embraces the act of giving as well as the force of being.[16]

15. Ibid., 10.

16. Bernard Beckerman, *Theatrical Presentation: Performer, Audience, and Act* (ed. Gloria Brim Beckerman and William Coco; New York: Routledge, 1990), 1.

Theatre, then, is an act of presentation that occurs through performance, which requires isolation and temporal control in order to bring performer, spectator, and the act of presentation into relationship with one another. In general, it is the performer whose presence makes the exchange unique. In many cases, Beckerman points out, the performer may be "completely identified with the act performed."[17] This is certainly true in the case of the prophets, whose oracles, visions, and prophecies are organized under their names. However, as closely as any performer may be identified with an act of presentation, the performer is not the act itself, but the medium through which the act is presented. This idea is critical to understanding the relationship between the prophet and the scribe, and the transition from the oral to the written tradition of the prophets. If the performer is not his or her act, "then what is there in a performer besides the act that is performed?"[18] Aside from the tradition of the prophet, what might the scribe have appropriated? In the reading and rereading of the prophetic text, as Ben Zvi suggests, what was "extracted" so it could be presented to an audience? Questions such as these are why an exploration of theatre-as-presentation must first be considered before the problems of "script." Before the scribes created the tradition of prophetic literature, the prophets created a tradition of presentation (a theatrical tradition). The "script" tends only to give a hint or suggestion of the activity to be performed. It is presentation that gives activity its concrete expression.[19]

As we proceed to an examination of prophetic literature and the tradition created by the scribes, it is necessary to understand the organic and interdependent nature of theatrical and dramatic activity. As Beckerman writes, "Aristotle initiated an unfortunate precedent in first compartmentalizing the six parts of tragedy and then rating them in degrees of importance. . . . He encouraged generations of critics to discriminate against the visual and kinesthetic aspects of theatre and to neglect the study of the interrelationship between the internal and external features of presentation."[20] The primary features we are concerned with here are the relationships between the

17. Ibid., 5.

18. Ibid., 7.

19. Beckerman, *Dynamics of Drama*, 13.

20. Ibid., 225.

performer and the audience and the act and the audience. The crux of these relationships is in the dramatic activity, activity which is embedded in the text. Apprehension of this activity requires what we are calling a *performance mode of thought* by both the presenter and the spectator. It is the performance mode of thought that allows the two to meet and mutually participate in the experience of the drama.

THEATRICAL TO DRAMATIC ACTIVITY

In editing our definitions of theatre and drama, presentation becomes the focal point. As Beckerman points out, all presentation is doing, and from the spectator's point of view, doing consists of a sequence of perceptible signs created by the performer.[21] In fact, activity is how the imagined act reaches the spectator. It is the medium that carries the message. In the full range of theatrical activity, these signs move across a continuum from the actual (what the presenter is doing) to the virtual (what the character is doing). Theatrical activity is the full range of motion possible that creates the appearance of what is perceived by the spectator. What appears as a result of the activity is an image to be apprehended by the spectator. The more the activity moves toward the virtual, the closer it moves toward dramatic activity and vice versa.[22] Take a halftime show by a marching band, for example. Clearly an act of presentation, this example of *theatrical activity* relies almost entirely on the *actual* ability of the members of the marching band to possess the skill to play their instruments and to execute the movement patterns on the field. What and how they perform is also structured to elicit certain responses from the spectators: usually applause and cheering, but not necessarily so. It is a presentation composed primarily of artificial elements: uniforms, instruments, flags, hats, and choreography, but it relies on the actual ability of the musicians to play and march simultaneously. Or, at the other end of the continuum,

---

21. Beckerman, *Dynamics of Drama*, 11. The role of the spectator is thoroughly explored in chapter 4. However, theatrical and dramatic presentations, as modes of communication, are always presented *to* an audience. The presence of spectators is an essential part of the presentation equation and is reflected in all the definitions and concepts the authors employ.

22. Beckerman adopts Suzanne Langer's notion of the term *virtual* here: "An image, something that exists only for perception, abstracted from the physical and causal order is the artist's creation. . . . Through the artist's efforts a new appearance has superseded [the] the natural aspect" of the raw materials, and the resulting image "is a purely virtual 'object.'" Beckerman, *Dynamics of Drama*, 16–17.

consider Charlton Heston in his most famous role, Moses in *The Ten Commandments*. Though a certain amount of ability of the kind required of the musicians is present in Heston's fight scenes, it is the work the actor does to bring forth the character that moves us into the virtual world of the drama. It is how well the actor plays the instruments of his own voice and body so that spectators "believe" in the virtual world presented to them that distinguishes the drama as a form of theatre.[23] It must have been the same with the Hebrew prophets. Their skillful presentation of the word of the Lord brought the spectators to that moment of belief.

The performance appears, as Beckerman would suggest, as an activity "devised and practiced by men to astonish and delight others."[24] On the continuum of theatrical and dramatic activity, we can place the marching band at the theatrical end. As Ben Zvi points out, the training in one's actual ability to read and proclaim the prophetic text was likely a part of the scribal process, which would also place oral presentation nearer the theatrical end of the spectrum, with the emphasis on theatrical activity (what the presenter does). However, the more the effort made by the scribe to create the world of the prophet, the more the presentation moves toward the dramatic end of the spectrum.

> As a mode of theatrical art, the medium of drama is not language, but human presence. Language, vital as it is to the art of the drama, is introduced through the activity of men speaking. But speaking is such a generalized form of activity, we must modify even that statement by stating that men conversing, men orating, and men reciting are among the activities, and therefore media, of drama. To understand drama, we must return to the source of drama, that is, to theatre. Theatre occurs. Therefore, as a subform of theatre, drama occurs. It too, is not a thing but a happening of a distinctive sort. Theatre occurs during presentation. So does drama. Drama too, occurs through the medium of human beings. . . . Yet drama differs from other forms of presenta-

23. See the glossary for a definition of "willing suspension of disbelief." This concept is also dealt with in chapter 4.

24. Beckerman, *Dynamics of Drama*, 14.

> tion in one major respect: The presentation of drama is a presentation of an imagined act.[25]

In the case of prophetic dramas, it was the scribe who moved the presentation along the continuum of theatrical and dramatic activity.

(Theatrical) ←——————————→ (Dramatic/Virtual)
(Actual) (Imagined Act)

The imagined act, which is produced by dramatic activity, is a difficult concept. It will be easier to explain the concept within the framework of what we traditionally recognize as "drama," and then to proceed to work backward from that example to the dramatic world of the prophets. The imagined act is what creates the crucial distinction of drama and dramatic activity from other forms of presentation. The imagined act includes both the performed behavior of the "actor" and the inner life that behavior reveals. Beckerman uses the phrase "imagined act" in an effort to avoid the Aristotelian notion of mimesis, or imitation, which is too closely linked to the Greek philosophical view of the relationship of literature to reality.[26] The creation of the imagined act in performance, rather than merely reflective of reality, includes both the construction and reconstruction of experience through the operation of the imagination. This distinction is necessary in order to understand both the prophetic act as well as the creation of the prophetic text by the scribes. As Levy writes of the passage from Samuel, "The passage clearly reveals a belief in the creative word, a conviction that language not only describes reality but also creates it."[27] And it is more than just verbal language in the case of theatre. It is all the languages of performance and presentation: language of the body, the space the body occupies, objects, clothing. These languages of the theatre and the drama have a highly focused purpose: to be seen.

The function of theatrical and dramatic activity is the creation of images that can be apprehended by spectators in the here and now of the presentation.

25. Ibid., 18.
26. Ibid., 19.
27. Levy, *Bible as Theatre*, 15.

> An actor presenting an imagined act is engaged in a double effort: the demonstration of actual skill and the portrayal of virtual existence. He demonstrates actual skill by the way he imitates natural behavior and constructs artificial activity simultaneously. In enacting a death scene, for instance, the actor must show how life leaves a body while he clearly articulates his words. What he imitates, often, is not actuality by a schematic notion of actuality that can be readily perceived by the audience. Breaking his normal rhythm of breathing is one way of indicating the onslaught of death. Originality comes not from absolute fidelity to nature but from a combination of freshly observed features of natural behavior with formal elements of presentation. By using schematic stage activity, he gives the appearance of inner life. This is the imagined act.[28]

More simply put, the use of schematic activity by the actor actually creates the appearance of inner life. What Beckerman is describing is a typical example of how an actor creates the imagined act of a character dying on stage in a scripted play. This example obviously relates to the fictional world of the drama as we know it from going to the theatre to see a play. However, the component elements of this "imagined act" constitute a schema for presentation that is applicable to the prophetic act of presenting an oracle or a vision. Again, we are talking about theatre and drama as mediums of presentation. In this schema, the prophet, as presented to us in the text, moves from being *actor* to being *character* by answering the Lord's call to prophesy. What he does as prophet constitutes the imagined act. For example, Amos's move from shepherd to prophet exemplifies the move from what the actor does to what the character does. Amos is still Amos, but must figure out how to present himself as prophet. We will later identify this as fulfilling his "project," but for now it is important to illustrate the nature of theatrical and dramatic activity in terms of how they move along a continuum. They are mutually dependent because of the human presence of the presenter. We have represented them below in a vertical rather than linear fashion because the

28. Beckerman, *Dynamics of Drama*, 18.

movement of dramatic activity is toward the revelation of the inner life of the drama. This movement requires a performance mode of thought from both presenters and spectators because the inner life is the *where* where the two connect.

Activity (what the actor does)

↓

Imagined act (what the character does)

↓

Inner life (what the imagined act reflects/reveals)

It is through activity that the character, imagined act, and inner life of the drama are created. This activity can only be carried out by a living being engaged in a double effort: "the demonstration of actual skill and the portrayal of virtual existence. He [the actor] demonstrates actual skill by the way he imitates natural behavior and constructs artificial activity simultaneously."[29] Amos cannot *act* as prophet by continuing to engage in the activities of a shepherd. He does not deliver his oracles against foreign nations while trading in sheep or caring for trees. In order to *become* the prophet, he must engage in new activities that help to create the character of the prophet in order to reveal the inner life of his prophetic activity. After having been called by God to prophesy, the prophet must construct a mode of communication. The oracles and visions given to him by God can only be delivered through some medium of communication that has real time and space connection with the spectators who need to hear these oracles and see these visions. However, for the inner life of these oracles and visions to be revealed, for their

29. Ibid.

connection to God to be made concrete, the prophet must transform the real time and space of the presentation into a virtual time and space where the inner life of the prophetic activity becomes real through the shared act of presentation.

Dramatic activity is an activity of appearance. Theatre historians recognize that plays constructed of patterns of dramatic activity, from the Athenian tragedy of the fifth century forward, use various modes of activity that become conventionalized by the historical era in which they are written. These patterns are drawn from myth, legend, romance, current events, or the fantastical. In the case of the scribes, the tradition of the prophets themselves, as well as the followers of the prophets and the activities they engaged in, provided an existing source of material.

The function of dramatic activity is to make something appear, to make it happen in front of spectators. How it happens in any one given historical period is determined by a number of forces, but most particularly by what spectators ultimately approve. Modes of dramatic activity, writes Beckerman, vary from age to age. Dramatic activity always represents a state of being, an idea, which in general cannot be revealed directly.[30]

> Thus, we find the Greek tragic propensity toward propitiation, debate (agon) and revelation (anagnorisis). Episode after episode employs these fundamental activities. The debate is found in The Orestia (between Clytemnestra and the elders after the murder of Agamemnon), in Oedipus (between Oedipus and Tiresias, although the entire play is a series of debates as is Antigone), and in the patriotic plays of Euripedes. Activities of propitiation and revelation occur in almost every Greek Tragedy.[31]

The prophetic tradition of oracles, visions, and revelations, a tradition that existed before the literary tradition and that makes the literary tradition possible, is also a tradition of presentation and performance rooted in certain patterns of dramatic activity. As David Stacey writes, "The dramas that we consider were performed by men who were recognized, not only in their day

30. Ibid., 21.

31. Ibid.

but in later times, to be prophets."[32] In asking the question of how prophetic drama differs from other dramatic action in the life of Israel, Stacey writes:

> There are several features that assist a definition. In the first place, and very obviously, it was carried out by peculiarly gifted people called prophets. Prophetic acts partake of the mysterious potency that is associated with prophecy in general. The study of significant acts in Israel suggests that the person who carries them out is all-important. There is little evidence that the action depends upon an impersonal technique, secret, subtle, difficult or whatever. On the contrary, the actions are usually straightforward and their effectiveness—however effectiveness is reckoned—derives from the dynamic nature of the person who carries them out.[33]

BUILDING A DRAMA

In the drama, writes Beckerman, the performer "enacts a sequence of action-blocks in such a way as to project their forms to an audience."[34] By perceiving the activity, the audience becomes involved in a give-and-take with the performer. Initially, the engagement of the audience "occurs between the physical activity of performance and the sensitized organs of perception in the audience. Gradually, the sensory response expands into the imaginative."[35] As this process occurs, initiated by the shape and rhythm of the dramatic activity, the question becomes: What is sustained between the spectators and performers? Or, what is sustained between the activity as it appears in the imagination and the listener or reader who imagine the drama playing itself out? In either case, of live or imagined performance, what we respond to is the *how*. We follow the shape of the activity and the path that shape creates. In the case of the prophetic acts, available to us through the text of the Bible, that shape has been created for us by the scribal process. The text supports our *seeing* it happen. The nature of dramatic activity is that it moves, evolves,

---

32. David Stacey, *Prophetic Drama in the Old Testament* (London: Epworth, 1990), 60.

33. Ibid.

34. Beckerman, *Dynamics of Drama*, 145.

35. Ibid.

and is always in a state of becoming. It is a total process of interaction involving perception, the sustaining of the imaginary, the experience of sensation, and the physical and mental adjustment to that sensation.[36] In order for this activity to become theatre, it must be presented. This is perhaps where Levy's identification of the book of Samuel as *potential* theatre is most useful. But it is more than the presence of the theatrical languages of props, lighting, setting, and movement that creates this potential. It is how theatre and drama function in relationship to the spectator, to the process of apprehension, that we need to explore.

If we use Levy's analysis of I Sam 3 as an example of how this total process of interaction occurs, the centrality of the relationship between dramatic activity and the spectator can be made more concrete.[37] The Lord calls Samuel three times, and each time the boy goes to Eli, thinking that it was Eli who called him. Eli sends him away each time, telling Samuel to go back and lie down. After the third time Samuel comes to him, Eli realizes that it is the Lord who is calling Samuel. Levy emphasizes the forward thrust of the drama and suggests how our interest and emotions might be affected by the shape and rhythm of the dramatic activity. We watch, even if only in our mind's eye, the mounting tension of Samuel's three approaches to Eli. We become increasingly involved in Samuel's confusion and Eli's loneliness, and experience with Eli the moment of realization that the Lord is calling Samuel. We experience Samuel's mounting anxiety, and our hearts must surely stop along with his when he comes face to face with the Lord. As Levy suggests, the path of the action enhances Eli's loneliness and isolation. But how can *we* know this? In live theatre, the actor is the most crucial creator of the signs that connect us to the activity. But we also know that a good storyteller or preacher can engage us in the emotional and psychological experience of these characters. We know that a powerful reading of a biblical text can create the sensations of something very "real" for us. The *how* is what we are concerned

36. Ibid., 149. In his chapter on theatrical presentation, Beckerman deals specifically with the act-audience relationship of live performance. However, the relationship between the presentation and the spectator Beckerman describes parallels the process that actors, directors, and designers go through when dealing with a script. The units of activity must be seen, sensed, and put together in the imagination, including the experience of sensation expected in the spectator.

37. Levy, *Bible as Theatre*, 30–31.On these pages, Levy breaks down the ten verses of the drama and describes the very kind of forward yearning that Beckerman identifies as the essential nature of the drama.

with. That is why we have turned to the *how* of performance as the model for understanding a performance mode of thought.

However, in the biblical text we do not have actual records of the prophetic traditions, but constructed versions of the lives and acts of the prophets. In this scenario, the scribe becomes the actor, and the prophet he presents to us is the character, just as Samuel himself, or Amos as we will see later in this book, is transformed from actor to character when functioning as prophet (at least within the pages of the Amos document). The following schematic helps to visualize this "doubling" process:

Samuel	↔	**Prophet**	↔	**Scribe**	↔	**Samuel**
(actor)		**(character)**		**(actor)**		**(character)**

Dramatic activity encompasses the entire range of presentation: mimetic, acrobatic, gymnastic, musical, gestural, oration, recitation, debate, and revelation. Dramatic activity is malleable, and can be combined in any number of ways to serve any number of purposes. "Normally, it [dramatic activity] is embedded in the dialogue of a script," says Beckerman, "though it may be described in a scenario or devised in rehearsal."[38] In the method of analysis we will employ, the focus is on the relationship between dramatic activity and the imagined act, or between what is explicit and implicit in the text that works to reveal the inner life of the drama. In order to recognize dramatic activity, Beckerman suggests the following questions:

- What is its connection with actuality?
- What skills are needed to perform it?
- What is its evocative potential?
- Why was it selected?
- How is it arranged (in the case of a script)?
- Against what historical or imaginative background will it be viewed?[39]

SCRIPT

It is clear that we cannot be concerned with all of these questions. We do not have the prophet before us providing us direct access to the presentation

38. Beckerman, *Dynamics of Drama*, 32.
39. Ibid., 33.

itself, nor do we have the scribe, readers, or rereaders of the text before us. However, as Stacey reminds us, people carried out prophetic activity and the primacy of that notion of activity must remain with us when considering any kind of drama. Activity, and the arrangement of that activity into segments, is the core of the drama. What we must do is focus on those questions that help us consider the relation between text and the activity the text is meant to represent. In this sense, the dramatic text is generally referred to as a "script." The dramatic script, writes Beckerman, is the most loosely woven of all forms of verbal expression. One of the most important distinctions between a dramatic text (script) and other forms of literature is absence. What is not there, or is merely implied in terms of activity, is key. When Shakespeare writes, "they fight," or "all exeunt," he reminds us that the *how,* or the shape of that activity, must be created by those engaged in its presentation.

> Between sentences and words room is left for human impulse to move toward and away from individuals or incipient events. A rhythm of intensification and decrescence is written into any competent script, and it is awareness of this rhythm that makes play reading enjoyable. By becoming sensitive to the open spaces in the dialogue, we begin to feel the gestures, the reactions, the pauses that they imply, and thus begin to sense the pattern of action.[40]

In reading and rereading, we perceive the action through the fragments of activity in the script and the way these fragments are arranged into segments. For simplicity's sake, we can talk about segments as the building blocks of what might be typically identified as a scene. In the traditional literary model of the drama, the play (script) is divided into acts and scenes, either by the playwright or by a dominant convention followed in a given period of history. The biggest limitation of this kind of division is that one scene will include multiple smaller units that tend to be ignored by the process of literary analysis. Breaking a scene into smaller units is usually the work of actors and directors who must think "performatively" in order to figure out how to play the scene in its moment by moment life on the stage. This kind of analytical

40. Ibid., 62.

work tends to be driven by acting methods, which are, by necessity, too limited in their scope for what we are proposing.[41]

The segment, as introduced by Beckerman, is a unit of the drama that includes all the spatiotemporal elements of the script and maintains a focus on the script as a series of events.[42] Rather than merely tracing a linear progression of the events, identification and analysis of segments seeks to discover patterns and inter-relationships among segments. Analysis of segments concerns both the script and the spaces between what's in the script. In this way, the relationship between the imagined act and the inner life of the drama is played out as part of the analysis.[43] If, as Ben Zvi writes, the authoritative texts of the scribes were the starting point for "oral performances" of the literati, it is reasonable to assume that their performances involved this relationship between, on the one hand, the activity of the prophets, God, and others present in the act, and on the other, an attempt to reveal the inner life of the drama to their spectators. In other words, the oral presenters were engaged in a performance mode of thought that allowed them to connect with their spectators in the imaginary time and space of the drama.

The dramatic segment, or basic unit of the drama, focuses attention on how the activity of the drama functions as the connector between performance and spectator. What follows are salient features of the segment, which will be useful points of reference for our later application to Amos and other prophetic scripts. Segments are the spatiotemporal units of dramatic activity that are arranged in the script through the process of selection and feedback the playwright imposes on the script. This process of selection and feedback, which we discussed earlier, determines the pattern of activity the characters engage in. It is the segment, or most basic unit of dramatic activity, and its relationship to the other segments of a script that provides the focal point for both imagining and playing the drama.

41. Perhaps we should point out that it may well be that the dramatic segments are responsible for some of the literary structures that eventually make their way to the prophetic documents. Consequently, literary criticism must be mindful of a performative mode of thought.

42. Both theatrical and dramatic segments are given extensive treatment in Beckerman's *Dynamics of Drama*. Our work focuses on the nature of the dramatic segment and is developed directly from Beckerman's concepts.

43. See the diagram on page 65.

Prophetic text	⟷	**Script**
Prophet	⟷	**Actor/Character**
Scribe	⟷	**Playwright/Actor**
Prophetic Acts	⟷	**Dramatic Activity**

DRAMATIC SEGMENTS

A dramatic segment is any coherent unit of time that nests within a formal dramatic unit, such as an act or scene. Dramatic segments have the following characteristics[44]:

- Their coherence must be determined by a thorough study of structure, and not merely by conventional means of denoting acts, scenes, or beats.
- Spectators experience a time-space relationship induced by the units of activity that are present in the script.
- Within this spatiotemporal frame, spectators perceive time as activity and through that perception enjoy a heightened sense of life.
- Performance occurs in an arranged sequence of events (plot) that has a time frame compatible with the existence of the time of the spectators. In other words, the time of the drama has a relationship to the time of "real" life. In prophetic dramas, revelation, initiation, vision, and transformation would have resonated with spectators because they occur in the "real" time of people's lives. For example, in the case of Levy's analysis of I Sam 3, the drama or revelation occurs late in the life of Eli, but in the youth of Samuel, and also over the course of a night, so that Samuel "awakens" the next morning and opens the doors of the temple.[45]

44. These characteristics are adapted from chapter 2 of Bernard Beckerman's *Dynamics of Drama*, 35–78.

45. Levy essentially uses I Sam 3:1–10 as a series of small scenes focused on the active verbs that drive the scene forward. His analysis comes very close to being segment based, but stops short of considering the full range of temporal and spatial questions of performance. Levy acknowledges that "verbs are the driving force of the drama," but does not extend his analysis into the virtual realm of dramatic activity. Levy, *Bible as Theatre*, 30–31.

- Simultaneously, the imagined act (the virtual world of the drama), observes its own time scheme, communicated through the dramatic activity. The virtual time scheme of the drama relates to the way we conceive time to pass. The classical tendency was to shape the imagined act to coincide with the duration of the presentation (the doctrine of the unity of time). Elizabethan theatre compressed a narrative time sequence of considerable time into two or three hours of performance time. The modern tendency has often been to expand a few moments of a life (a dream, an instance of memory) into an evening's presentation. The time of the prophetic drama seems to vary whether we are talking about a call narrative, a revelation, an oracle, or a vision.
- A rhythm of involvement and disengagement is a mandatory aspect of dramatic segments. Both performer and spectator impose meaning on the experience by the way major and minor signs are designated. In oral presentations, this could have included tone of voice, volume, pauses, and even gestures. By employing a performance mode of thought, the reader of the prophetic text can envision the full range of activity suggested in the text. The result of this process is a series of activity-defined segments rather than a linear description of a plot sequence.

The function of dramatic activity is to make something appear, something that can be apprehended by the spectator. Because dramatic activity is an act of presentation, it is governed by the interplay between spectator and presentation. In live theatre, the actor largely governs this interplay; however, this interplay can also be governed by the reader, or rereader, as well as by the scribe, who governed the process of selection in the arrangement of the prophetic texts we have available to us. What all of these participants share is a performance mode of thought, a dramatic imagination, if you will, that allows the drama to take shape. The drama takes shape through the arrangement of segments, segments of activity that propel both the "actor" and the spectator toward a future point.

I SAMUEL 3: PERFORMANCE MODE OF THOUGHT

With dramatic activity, we have two planes of immediate experience presented to us: "the activity actually presented to us containing the form and attitude of the author/creator and the historical act from which it is drawn."[46] This is precisely what Levy describes in the case of Samuel's initiation:

> The author of the Book of Samuel presumably understood the narrative as not only a literary text but also as an historically accurate account, or, at least, a story which follows the description of a hero. Consequently, and also due to the author's literary knowledge and skill, the way the message is conveyed is less prominent than the message itself.[47]

For this reason, Levy suggests, the passage can be regarded as "potential theatre, as something that constituted a 'scene' when it occurred and that can be reconstructed as theatre."[48] To do this, Levy employs the text along with the theatrical languages of props, set design, and so forth. Levy uses the text to engage in a performance mode of thought in order to "reconstruct" the scene from Samuel. Though he uses different tools, he moves from what the characters do (the *imagined acts* of God, Eli, and Samuel) to what those activities reflect (the *inner life* of this drama of revelation).

By placing primary emphasis on the verbs employed in the text, Levy suggests that the words have a performative function, that "verbs indicating speech must be considered descriptions of deeds and have the same status as action verbs."[49] If we take Levy's example and extend his work further by looking at I Sam 3 as segmented dramatic activity, a whole new set of questions emerges that begins to imagine how this scene can be played as well as how it might have actually been played in the life of the prophet.[50] The first task in such an analysis is to identify the explicit activity provided by the text and then to ask questions about the implicit activity, or the potential *how* of

46. Beckerman, *Dynamics of Drama,* 58.

47. Levy, *Bible as Theatre,* 15.

48. Ibid.

49. Ibid., 31.

50. James Linville comes very close to describing these concepts when writing about the narrative in chapter 7 of Amos: "The third-person voice of the narrative comes from somewhere other than Amos, the recipient of the visions. This other voice relates a story concerning the empirical world, not the mysterious encounters with the divine which mark the vision reports. Yet, in the story's incompleteness and the distancing of its ostensibly objective narrative voice, it appears as dream-like and as surreal as the visions. The author leaves much to the imagination." Linville, "Visions and Voices: Amos 7–9," *Biblica* 80 (1999): 33.

the activity. The two columns below establish the explicit activity that Levy identifies from the text, and we have added the column of implicit activity that begins to ask performative questions. By operating in this performance mode of thought, the potential inner life of the drama begins to take shape. The script provides the starting place for conjuring the life of the drama whether one is a reader, rereader, or actor in the drama.

Explicit Activity	Implicit Activity
Eli lies in his usual place. The lamp of God has not yet gone out. Samuel lies down in the temple. The Lord calls Samuel.	Does Samuel hesitate to see if it was really Eli's voice? Does he look around the room to try and orient himself? Is he fearful that something may be wrong with Eli?
Samuel answers. Samuel runs to Eli and speaks to him. Eli answers that he did not call Samuel and tells him to lie down, which Samuel does.	Does Samuel hesitate before he speaks? Is Eli startled to see him? Does Eli pause to study Samuel, who has just run to him? Does Samuel leave immediately? Does he lie down and go right back to sleep?
The Lord calls a second time. Samuel runs to Eli. Eli answers that he did not call Samuel and tells him to lie down, which Samuel does. Eli orders Samuel back to bed. The Lord calls Samuel a third time.	When awakened a second time, is Samuel frantic? Is Eli startled to see him again? Do the two hesitate in speaking? Does either show signs of anxiety or impatience? Does Eli try comforting Samuel? As Samuel leaves, does Eli return immediately to sleep? How do they address each other by the third visit?
Eli realizes that the Lord is calling Samuel. He tells Samuel to lie down and how to answer if the Lord calls again.	How does Eli show his realization that the Lord is calling Samuel? Does he share this directly with Samuel, or hesitate? Are they looking at each other for this exchange? Where is Samuel looking when Eli tells him how to answer? Does Samuel hesitate? Show signs of fear? How long does he pause before leaving Eli?

Explicit Activity	Implicit Activity
Samuel returns to his place and the Lord calls him again. Samuel answers as Eli instructed him. The Lord tells Samuel what he will do to the house of Eli.	Is he lying down when the Lord calls this time? Where is he looking? Does he hesitate before answering the Lord? Does he answer with full voice? Where does he look while the Lord speaks? Does he tremble at what will happen to the house of Eli? How does Samuel pass the time until morning? Does he pause before opening the doors? Does he look for Eli?
Samuel lies down until morning and then gets up to open the doors of the house of the Lord. Samuel is afraid to tell Eli what the Lord has said. Eli calls Samuel to him, asks what the Lord said, and threatens Samuel to tell him everything. Samuel reveals everything to Eli.	Does Samuel tense up when Eli calls him? Is Samuel able to look Eli in the face? Does he shrink back from Eli's threat? Does he look at Eli when reporting what the Lord has told him? Is his voice flat? Is it tense? Does Samuel's body seem to apologize for delivering the message? Where does Eli look when Samuel speaks? Is he sitting or standing?
Eli answers, "It is the LORD; let him do what seems good to him."	Is Eli looking at Samuel when he proclaims the Lord's goodness?

By examining the relationship between the explicit and the implicit activity, the other key features of dramatic activity begin to emerge more concretely. What is typically referred to as the rising and falling action of the drama, or what we refer to as a rhythm of involvement and disengagement, is revealed by the direction the explicit activity suggests and the possibilities of how that activity occurs as suggested by the implicit activity. The explicit activity of I Sam 3 suggests that by the third time Samuel comes to Eli, thinking that Eli has called him, a certain amount of tension has developed that results in Eli's realization that it is the Lord calling Samuel. Some of this tension is dispersed when Eli tells Samuel what is happening and gives him direction for what to do. However, at the same time, the tension shifts to Samuel, who must wait for the Lord to call him. The tension begins to mount again after the Lord speaks to Samuel because what the Lord has revealed to him puts Samuel in conflict with Eli. This kind of linear tracking of the tension and conflict reinforces the structural nature of dramatic activity. Each unit of this "segment" presents us with coherent bits of time (both actual and virtual), nesting within the formal dramatic unit of I Sam 3.

However, it is the implicit activity that most concerns us in terms of demonstrating a performance mode of thought. Through the implicit activity, it becomes immediately apparent that we are concerned with more than the plot. The implicit activity involves the actions and reactions of Eli and Samuel, as well as the suggested presence of the Lord. Interrelationships become the focus of the implicit activity. The possible gestures, movements, glances, and avoidances begin to put flesh on the bones of the activity, deepening our sense of the rhythm of the drama, including potential pauses, which are significant moments of nonverbal exchange. The implicit activity begins to suggest the rhythm and shape of the space between the explicit activity, the act itself, and the spectators. Exploring the implicit activity is how we engage with the imagined act, in order to connect with the inner life of the drama. In live performance, it is what the actor does (how the actor moves, speaks, turns, handles objects) that fulfills some of the possibilities of the implicit activity. No one performance can include all the possible ways an act can be performed. Without the presence of the actor, either in the creation of a script, or in the reading of a script, it is the interplay between explicit and implicit activity that leads us to the other properties of the drama as well. In other words, outside of our engagement with live performance of one kind or another, a performance mode of thought makes it possible for us to identify the elements of the drama and to see how they function as drama. We can do this by asking the following questions:

- What is the precipitating context? What information is supplied beforehand that establishes the circumstances of the segment?
- What is the project of each character? What is the character moving toward, focusing his energy toward?
- What path does the tension follow? What kinds of resistance are present to provide increases and decreases in the tension?
- Where is the crux of the segment (intensification-relaxation pattern as opposed to the issue-decision pattern of "crisis"[51])? When does the rhythm of the segment reach maximum intensification? What happens following that moment?

The process of answering these questions provides a total image of the drama rather than a description of the parts of the drama.

PRECIPITATING CONTEXT

What we know of what happened before a segment begins provides the precipitating context.[52] For the spectator, this information can come both from the script (as the drama unfolds) and from the spectator's relationship to the tradition from which the drama is constructed. As Levy indicates, the first two chapters of I Samuel establish a pattern leading to the encounter between God, Eli, and Samuel in chapter 3. The directionality of the preceding chapters is something we will look at as the project, or the movement forward of the characters toward a projected end. If, as Levy suggests, chapter 3 is an initiation scene—"a bar mitzvah, or confirmation"[53]—for Samuel, then our question is what information comes before chapter 3 that helps establish the grounds for our understanding of it as an initiation segment? What happens before the initiation segment that links to the activity of the segment we are analyzing?

Levy identifies two triangular patterns of activity between the House of Elkanah and the House of Eli that represent "two future alternatives—service to God against failure to serve God."[54] Levy writes, "It is clear that

51. Beckerman, *Dynamics of Drama,* 51.

52. In terms of performance criticism, this is the function of the introductions found in the prophetic books.

53. Levy, *Bible as Theatre,* 15.

54. Ibid., 23.

among these triangles God prefers the House of Elkanah over the House of Eli."[55] In what follows, Levy identifies eighteen encounters in the first two chapters that set the stage for chapter 3. His analysis of these eighteen encounters is based on the idea that the "dramatic quality of a text derives from the dialogues it contains."[56] We certainly agree that this is partially the case, but from the point of view of segments as the primary unit of dramatic action, the dialogues do not provide all the dramatic quality. However, Levy's reading of the script helps make the idea of the precipitating context clear.

By the time we get to chapter 3, where Samuel is ministering to the Lord under Eli's supervision, the circumstances of Samuel's initiation become clear. It is the oracle against Eli that provides the immediate precipitating context for the segment that follows in chapter 3. In light of the oracle, we know that the Lord has promised that "a time is coming when I will cut off your strength and the strength of your ancestor's family, so that no one in your family will live to old age" (1 Sam 2:31). The very first verse of chapter 3 immediately suggests to us that that time has indeed come: "The word of the LORD was rare in those days; visions were not widespread." The delivery of the oracle by a man of God at the end of chapter 2 followed by the Lord calling Samuel almost the instant we enter the activity of chapter 3 is a perfect example of how dramatic segments link to each other not simply by causality (A makes B happen) but as a process of growing together into a whole. The delivery of the oracle against Eli at the end of chapter 2 does not make the Lord appear to Samuel in chapter 3. However, the delivery of the oracle against Eli at the end of chapter 2 does make the appearance of the Lord in chapter 3 a clear part of a growing whole. "Linear intensification is simply the inherent requirement of any theatrical situation," says Beckerman.[57] Our identification of the precipitating circumstances as we move from segment to segment is critical to developing a clear sense of the shape of the action. What is generating the activity directly, as opposed to elements of the

---

55. Ibid.

56. On pages 22–29 of *Bible as Theatre*, Levy provides a thorough analysis of the drama from the point of view of the verbal and explicit nonverbal moments. Levy's descriptions provide an excellent map of these moments, and our work here is meant to extend Levy's analysis beyond the explicit and linear aspects of the drama by describing ways that one can slice vertically into these moments to develop a deeper image of the drama.

57. Beckerman, *Dynamics of Drama*, 50.

drama that may have other purposes? The more clearly we identify the precipitating circumstances, the more clearly we are able to think about the explicit activity of a segment in terms of the implicit activity that gives the drama life.

PROJECT

Once we have examined the precipitating context and circumstances for a segment, we need to look carefully at what the characters are doing within that context. In Beckerman's theory of analysis, this is an examination of the characters' *projects.*

> In introducing the term "project," I am departing from common usage. It seems necessary to do so in order to distinguish accurately how human energy is expended through activity. Every segment, as we know, has an impelling force of some sort. Customarily this force is termed "drive" or "motivation." Actors speak of what characters "want" or of their "action," that is, the purpose of their activity. Their usage, however, is but one part of the larger concept of project. . . . To illustrate the point on a simple level, I can speak of a man wanting to make money. However, to know that man I would have to know his project. One cannot live out the abstract purpose of wanting to make money, only the concrete project. The urge to make money may manifest itself in one's imagination and behavior negatively, that is, as escaping poverty one has known, or positively, as owning a yacht or walking into an exclusive hotel. It is such a way that the project is the concrete focal point of a character's energy, and it is the project that the performer enacts.[58]

The idea of a "project" includes many kinds of energy that humans exert. "At one extreme," writes Beckerman, "we have determined efforts to achieve

58. Beckerman, *Dynamics of Drama,* 70.

a specific goal. At the other, generalized impulses."[59] The totality of a character's energy can be considered "motivation." When a character's energy is conscious and specific, it can be identified as "intention." These distinctions are important to make because a character's energy can be rational, irrational, defined, vague, conscious, or unconscious.[60] In the triangle of Eli, Samuel, and the Lord, the project of each is significantly different, both in terms of motivation and intention. From the oracle delivered in chapter 2, the project most clear is that of the Lord. First Samuel 2:26—"Now the boy Samuel continued to grow both in stature and in favor with the LORD and with the people"—coupled with the oracle, leaves little doubt that the Lord's project is to replace Eli with Samuel.

Observing again that the project is the concrete focal point of a character's energy, both Eli and Samuel become very interesting characters. The precipitating circumstances, resonating with the oracle against Eli, present us with a clearly playable set of circumstances at the beginning of chapter 3, even without the narrative addition concerning the rarity of visions "in those days." We know it is sometime in the night, both literally and figuratively in terms of Eli's reality. Eli is lying down in his room, while Samuel is lying down in the temple. Based on the events that have occurred in the drama to this point, and the proximity of the oracle against Eli to the start of chapter 3, it becomes clear that Eli's project is to wait—wait for the oracle to come true. In the case of Eli, waiting for the oracle to come true is both his motivation and his intention. Things are different with Samuel. The ambiguity of Samuel's project, and the changes it is about to undergo, is the source of the tension in this drama. The changes in Samuel's motivation and intention are what provide the dynamics and make chapter 3 a functional segment in terms of dramatic activity.

As the dramatic activity of this segment occurs, Samuel's project is not to fulfill the mode of prophetic behavior. Based on the fact that he runs to Eli twice saying, "Here I am, for you called me," it would appear that Samuel's project is to serve Eli. Samuel has no idea that some other project

59. Beckerman, *Dynamics of Drama*, 71.

60. Even when considering the variety of projects encountered in prophetic literature, one cannot assume that all prophets, all prophetic acts, or all the other "characters" involved in these dramas share precisely the same project. In fact, the potential difference in project is very important to our exploration of the relationship between scribe, text, and audience.

awaits him. On his third trip to Eli, it is Eli who, fulfilling his own project of waiting for the oracle to come true, recognizes that Samuel's project has a new direction. In acknowledgment that his wait is over, Eli tells Samuel what he must do to take up this new project. If we look back at the explicit and implicit activity lists above in light of our discussion of precipitating circumstances and projects, the potential questions and possible modes of behavior for the implicit activity become even more alive. Imagine the moment that Eli realizes the Lord is calling Samuel. Clearly this moment is much more than what is explicitly stated. What does this realization encompass for Eli? Before he tells Samuel what to say should the Lord appear again, how does he look at Samuel? Does he look away from Samuel? Do Eli's eyes follow Samuel out of the room? This drama of initiation also becomes a drama of fulfillment, of rejection, of transformation, and of farewell. Samuel must now fulfill the mode of prophetic behavior. His first test comes immediately following his initiation. Samuel's meeting with Eli after opening the temple doors brings us to the crux of this drama.

Recall that the crux of a drama is somewhat different than the notion of crisis. As Beckerman points out, "In dramatic criticism crisis has normally suggested a moment of decision, and, although many a crux is such a moment, there are as many others in which the extremity of intensification is not expressed in a shift of direction so much as in a subsidence of tension."[61] The crux of a drama can also be a sustained period of intensification created by multiple forces, rather than being a single character's decision. The idea of crux places more emphasis on the flow of action, or the accumulative effect of the dramatic activity than on moments of character decision. A sustained period of intensity is precisely what is presented to us in the final moments of I Sam 3. From the moment Eli realizes that it is the Lord appearing to Samuel, to the moment Samuel reveals everything to Eli, a sustained level of intensity occurs. The dynamics of this intensity are modulated by explicit activity: Samuel returns to his bed for the third time, the Lord appears and tells Samuel what he will do to Eli, Samuel waits for morning, Samuel opens the doors of the temple, and he is called to Eli to reveal what the Lord has told him. It is not until Eli says, "It is the LORD; let him do what seems good to him," that a shift from tension to decrescence

61. Beckerman, *Dynamics of Drama*, 51.

occurs. Though all the lines of tension point to the change in Samuel's project, or to his initiation as a prophet, our analysis of the drama must be sure to include an image of the whole as it progresses.

The script of I Sam 3 presents us with Eli, Samuel, and the Lord. Implicit in the script is the idea that we can see Eli and Samuel, though separated in space. We are able to watch Samuel go to Eli three times. We are present with Samuel when the Lord speaks to him. We see him throw open the temple doors in the morning as well as seeing Eli call him for the final time. We witness Samuel's approach to Eli and his struggle to share with Eli all that the Lord has revealed to him. The script presents us with much more than the linear progression of what happens. Through a performance mode of thought, like that used by the scribe in the creation of the text, we are able to imagine this drama. Though we cannot reconstruct the actual "performances" of the prophets, an understanding of the nature of theatrical and dramatic activity is essential to an understanding of how prophetic texts can be read for their performative qualities.

CHAPTER FOUR

Amos: A Prophetic Performance

IS ALL THE WORLD A STAGE?

In his book *Prophetic Drama in the Old Testament,* David Stacey gives considerable attention to the problem of how to understand prophetic dramatic acts.[1] He rightly observes that prophetic dramatic acts are intended to affect reality beyond the scope of the act itself. But the exact nature of that interplay between two realms (the dramatic act and the "outside reality") is difficult to understand. Some have used the term "ecstasy" to describe this relationship between the prophet and the supernatural as well as the form of delivery that the prophet used to speak to a listening audience.[2] Others have described the prophetic dramatic acts as magic, because the power of the act can alternately be thought to seek to control the deity or be inspired by the deity.

Unsatisfied with the description of prophecy as magic, Stacey nonetheless recognizes that a power relationship exists between the prophetic action and

1. David Stacey, *Prophetic Drama in the Old Testament* (London: Epworth, 1990).

2. In a slightly different twist, a number of scholars examined the prophetic movement as an "ecstatic" movement that involved the supernatural overpowering of the prophetic messenger. See, for example, G. Holscher, *Die Propheten: Untersuchungen zur Religionsgeschichte Israels* (Leipzig: Hinrich, 1914); and J. Lindblom, *Prophecy in Ancient Israel* (Philadelphia: Fortress, 1962).

the broader reality: "Prophetic action and the reality which it relates participate in each other."[3] In making the claim of mutually participating realities, we think Stacey rightly also dismisses the word *symbol* as sufficient to explain the nature of the prophetic action.[4] When Isaiah walked barefoot and naked through the streets of Jerusalem, he was not just symbolizing the coming devastation but was participating in it and calling his audience to share in the experience of devastation.

In rejecting the terms *magic* and *symbol* as descriptors of the prophetic action, Stacey is forced to look further for a word that seems to fit the whole complex of prophetic behavior. He settles on the word *drama* to describe what the prophets were about. He offers this as a working definition: A drama is an act or action, that paired to a reality is, "the event or truth or condition to which the prophetic drama relates or draws attention."[5] Figuring out just how the drama and that other reality relate to one another can be difficult indeed, but credit must be given to Stacey for drawing our attention to the whole idea of two worlds or two realities that meet when the prophet begins his dramatic work.

We think Stacey is on the right track, but we want to modify his observations and see if we can carry the work a bit further. The acts and actions that Stacey describes as *drama,* we propose to label *performance.* The realm of the prophetic act, action, or speech we will now label the *performative space-time,* and the reality that it affects we will call simply the *real space-time* (although this term does not in any fashion denigrate the "realness" of the performative). As a starting point for investigating how the performative world of the prophets influenced the real world, we will now suggest that a paradigm be drawn from theatre. How does a theatrical performance wield influence over an audience? How does a theatrical production effect changes in the world outside the stage?

There is one line of scholarship that has hinted at a performative aspect to the prophetic action by focusing interest in the social location of the prophetic performance, at least as applied to a portion of the book of Amos. Several scholars have attempted to reconstruct what may have been a widely practiced social event: the *marzeah feast.* In these reconstructions, the

3. Stacey, *Prophetic Drama in the Old Testament,* 20.
4. Ibid., 21–22.
5. Ibid., 22.

marzeah feast was a "celebration sponsored by wealthy fraternal associations, documentation for which covers several centuries and a wide geographical area."[6] This feast, it has been suggested, lies behind the prophetic condemnations of Amos 2:7–8[7] and 6:1–4.[8] The final word has not yet been written on the social location of the Amos pronouncements, but what is sure is that the prophet did make oral pronouncements that wielded such power as to result in a traditional body of material that eventually made its way into the document that bears his name. In this chapter, we introduce several more performance criticism concepts and make application of those concepts to the book of Amos, its structure and flow.

CREATED TIME

One of the fascinating characteristics of performance is that it creates its own space and time. During the performance, the performer and audience are caught up in a reality of their own making—performance space-time. This performance space-time is invested with power by residents of real space-time but with the ability to act upon and change real space-time. The power of a performance is judged by its effects on the participants (actors and audience alike) once they leave the theatre.[9] This dynamic interplay between performance space-time and real space-time helps explain the use of time in both the Israelite cult and prophetic movement.[10]

6. Carroll R., M. Daniel, *Amos: The Prophet and His Oracles* (Louisville, Ky.: Westminster John Knox, 2002), 20.

7. See Hans Barstad, *The Religious Polemics of Amos: Studies in the Preaching of Amos 2, 7B–8; 4, 1–13; 5, 1–27; 6, 4–7; 8, 14* (Leiden: Brill, 1984).

8. See Phillip King, *Amos, Hosea, Micah: An Archaeological Commentary* (Philadelphia: Westminster, 1988), 137–61. See also Robert Coote, *Amos among the Prophets: Composition and Theology* (Philadelphia: Fortress, 1981), 36–39; and J. Alberto Soggin, "Amos and Wisdom," in *Wisdom in Ancient Israel* (ed. J. Day et al.; Cambridge: Cambridge University Press, 1995).

9. In some ways, this aspect of performance is similar to how anthropologists have described ritual. Mary Douglas likens ritual to currency. It is valuable and useful only when it enjoys public confidence. Once that confidence is lost, the currency is worthless. Douglas, *Purity and Danger* (London: Routledge & Kegan Paul, 1966), 37. Ritual may not change the surrounding events, but it changes the participants in the events. Performance space-time operates in a similar fashion. The performance does not change the event in the real space-time, but it changes the audience—the participants in the performance space-time who in turn have the potential to change events in real space-time.

10. Robinson called this performance space-time "representative realism." H. W. Robinson, "Hebrew Sacrifice and Prophetic Symbolism," *Journal of Theological Studies* 43 (1942): 129–39.

One of the interesting questions that has perennially arisen in biblical studies is the matter of understanding how cultic acts, or prophetic acts and statements, involving reference to the distant past or future were to affect the present. Some have suggested a sympathetic type of magic was at work. Others have considered these references as merely symbolic. Arthur Weiser represents a majority opinion within biblical studies: "The cultural ritual . . . concentrates the whole range of events in the single moment of the cultic act, so that the past, present and the future coincide."[11] Stacey's work also suggests that this description of the cultic ritual is applicable to the "telescoping of time" found in the Hebrew prophets as well.[12] Perhaps a better way of thinking about the issue is to consider the paradigm of performance space-time and real space-time. These two dimensions are intimately related and each is susceptible to the power of the other.

Performance space-time is woven into the biblical use of the Exodus tradition. An example of this dynamic relationship between real space-time and performance space-time can be found in the biblical instructions on keeping Passover in Exod 12–13. In the Passover celebration, the celebrant experiences the flight from Egypt and God's miraculous provision of release and liberation. Several things happen at once:

1. In the original flight from Egypt (or at least its memory in a historical context), real space-time provided the reason, structure, and meaning for the performance in performance space-time.
2. The performance space-time allowed the celebrant to participate in, experience, and benefit from an event in the distant real space-time. In a sense, real space-time—for the celebrant—was changed, allowing the celebrant to live an event while in performance space-time that may have occurred centuries ago in real space-time.
3. The function of performance space-time was to have an impact, to exert power on real space-time. After the celebration was over, it became a sign and a remembrance "so that the teaching of the LORD may be on your lips" (Exod 13:9).

---

11. Arthur Weiser, *Psalms* (Old Testament Library; trans. Herbert Hartwell; Philadelphia: Westminster, 1962), 44.

12. Stacey, *Prophetic Drama in the Old Testament*, 51.

It is fascinating to see that, in the biblical record, the instructions for the performance are partnered with an injunction for parents to instruct their children as to what this "means" (Exod 12:14, 17, 42; 13:8–10, 14). This instruction, given not in the performance but in real space-time, gives legitimacy to the performance space-time and allows the performance space-time to have power in real space-time.

The very same dynamic is at work in Deut 6:4–9. The pronouncement of the "Shema" is given as the reason for a reported performance that includes teaching, binding, and writing for the benefit of future generations. Likewise, the Decalogue is presented in performance space-time: "And God said" begins the recitation in both Exod 20 and Deut 5. But it is when the performance is over, when God finishes speaking, that the real power is evident. When the audience returns to real space-time, the performance exerts its real power.

Rather than time on a continuum of past-present-future, we need to think of the prophetic presentation of two dimensions of time and space: the real space-time of the ordinary and mundane and the performance space-time in which God is present and the supernatural is commonplace. The two dimensions are intimately related. Performance space-time is dependent upon real space-time, but real space-time is susceptible and influenced by the power of performance space-time.

Application of this performance principle can be made quite easily to the prophetic document. In Amos 3:1, the prophet makes reference to the exodus event. Amazingly, the address uses the second person form of speech: "Hear this word that the LORD has spoken against you, O people of Israel, against the whole family that I brought up out of the land of Egypt." Quite literally, the biblical story line places the event hundreds of years before the prophet and his audience. Yet the prophet is quite clear that they, the immediate audience, were the objects of God's liberation. Stacey, although admittedly not referring to this passage in Amos, draws an inference relative to his investigation of prophetic drama by stating, "If an event can be encountered in its dramatic representation, then it can be so encountered before it happens, just as easily as afterwards."[13] It is not the "before" or "after" that matter so much as it is the interplay between performance and real space-time. The prophet was quite skilled at managing the

13. Ibid., 55.

interplay between the two in order to accomplish his desired goal.[14]

PERFORMANCE SPACE-TIME AND FALSE PROPHECY

The Bible places more emphasis on identifying "false prophecy" than it does on identifying "false prophets."[15] That is, the concern was on distinguishing between a true and false act of prophecy rather than the trueness or falseness of the prophet. A true prophet could give a false prophecy and vice versa.[16] False prophecy was identified as having been commissioned by someone other than the Lord, God of Israel. And the only test was to wait and see if the prophecy influenced real space-time. In other words, if the performance space-time does not impact the real space-time, it is judged to be false. Zedekiah and Micaiah of I Kgs 22 provide wonderful examples of this principle at work. Zedekiah performs at the behest of Baal (or, maybe better, Ahab), and although he gives a wonderful performance, he is judged unreliable by Jehoshaphat and the writer of the account. Micaiah, on the other hand, speaks only "whatever the LORD says to me" (I Kgs 22:14). Yet it is not until having been vindicated by the power of performance space-time in real space-time that Micaiah is credited as having delivered a true prophecy (I Kgs 22:28).

The same concern is evident in Amos. In Amos 7, a narrative is given that contains the essence of a confrontation between Amos and Amaziah (7:10–17). Amaziah complains that Amos is, quite literally, out of place. Amaziah is upset because Amos is performing in the king's sanctuary, a temple of the kingdom. His admonition is for the prophet to go elsewhere—to go back to Judah and there to ply his trade. The essence of Amaziah's complaint is that there is too great a distance between the real space-time of Bethel in the mid-eighth century and the performance space-time of the prophet. Amos's created reality is just too big of a stretch for the comfort of Amaziah. The prophet replies, however, not on the condition of real space-

14. Within the scholarly literature on the prophets, renewed interest is being expressed in the function of the introductions to the prophetic documents. The introduction sets the stage for a prophetic document by locating the prophet in a time and place. It may be that the two realms—performance space-time and real space-time—find their boundary in these introductions. The introductions frame the world in which the prophetic performance is about to take place.

15. Stacey, *Prophetic Drama in the Old Testament*, 69.

16. To be sure, however, the prophet also could be considered false if he or she regularly acted on behalf of someone other than the Lord, God of Israel.

time but on the power of performance space-time. Despite Amaziah's discomfort, the prophet can only act according to the direction and the word of the Lord. In other words, Amos wants real space-time to be impacted by performance space-time, but Amaziah has no desire for the power of Amos's performance to influence life as he knows it. It is the clash of two dimensions, the real and the performed, that resides at the heart of the dispute in chapter 7.

IMPLEMENTS USED IN PERFORMANCE SPACE-TIME

One last characteristic of performance space-time must be considered. Performance space-time has a very permeable boundary. That is, performers are not always cast in their role but can jump back and forth between performance space-time and real space-time. Likewise, implements used in performance are not forever locked in a performance dimension but are able to reenter the world of the mundane without any necessary change in them. This is a distinguishing mark between the prophetic performance and the realm of cultic ritual. In cultic ritual, the implement changes and becomes devoted to that cultic use. The implement takes on the characteristics of the cultic reality and loses its presence in real space-time. Not so in a performance space-time. In a performance space-time there is no necessary connection between the implement and the performance reality. In the performance, the relationship between the implement and the performance reality is not permanent, and the object does not acquire the properties of the performance space-time, thereby allowing its use in real space-time.

AUDIENCE

In any discussion of performance criticism, a word must be said about the presence of an audience. A performer has no ability to affect an audience without the permission of that audience. The actor is dependent upon the will of the audience. Yet it is the project of the actor that transforms a crowd into an audience. A symbiotic relationship exists between the two. What is it then about the performance of the prophet or the scribe that assists in the transformation of a crowd into an audience?

Those familiar with the various literary methods applied to biblical studies might well suspect that reader-response insights are important in describing the function of the audience in performance criticism. Reader-response and reception theory, though abundant in literary studies, have had comparatively little impact on theatre studies, observes Marvin Carlson. This is largely the result of a tendency to examine the text and the performance, but not the reception of the performance.[17] Though this has started to change in more recent years, Carlson observes:

> The rather extensive reader-response and reception bibliography of the past decade or so suggests a number of potentially useful strategies for analyzing contemporary and historical theatre experience. We might consider, for example, the process of concretization as discussed by Wolfgang Iser—the process by which, according to Iser, a reader serves as coproducer of the meaning of a text by creatively filling gaps (*Leerstellen*) left in the text by the author. Those familiar with recent semiotic theory may recall that Anne Ubersfeld has described the dramatic text in particular as *troué*, that is containing gaps, in this case to be filled by staging.[18]

Carlson also points to the work of Hans Robert Jauss and the empirical disposition of the audience/readers provided by a "horizon of expectations."[19] The three factors upon which the horizon of expectations are based are the norms or immanent poetics of the genre, the implicit relationships to other familiar work, and opposition between fiction and reality.

These factors are essential to our exploration of the scribe-spectator relationship, and they also appear in Bernard Beckerman's work on the structure of dramatic activity and audience response. As Carlson suggests, "Generic expectations and relationship to other works (intertextuality) are clearly as relevant to theatre reception as to reading, and the juxtaposition of fiction and reality perhaps even more relevant, given the particularly central

17. Marvin Carlson, "Theatre Audiences and the Reading of the Performance," in *Interpreting the Theatrical Past: Essays in the Historiography of Performance* (ed. Thomas Postlewait and Bruce McConachie; Iowa City: University of Iowa Press, 1991), 82–98.

18. Ibid., 82–83. Carlson cites in this passage Wolfgang Iser, *Die Appelstruktur der Texte* (Constance: Druckerei und Verlagsanstalt Konstanz, 1970), 15; and Anne Ubersfeld, *Lire le Theatre* (Paris: Editions Sociales, 1977), 24.

19. Carlson, "Theatre Audiences and the Reading of the Performance," 83. See Hans Robert Jauss, *Toward an Aesthetic of Reception* (trans. Timothy Bahti; Minneapolis: University of Minnesota Press, 1982), 22–23, 25.

role played by mimesis and inconicity in the theatre."[20] However, much of the work in theatre studies that has been done on the problem of audience response and audience relationship to the performance has been largely semiotic. Though Carlson made this observation a decade ago, it remains true.

Working from Umberto Eco's concepts of the model reader and open and closed texts, Marco De Marinis theorizes the dramaturgy of the spectator: a dialectical balance between the pleasure of discovery, recognition, and the anticipated.[21] As De Marinis suggests, *dramaturgy* and *spectator* are not usually terms seen as connected. In order to establish his argument, he offers the following definitions:

> Dramaturgy: This may be defined as the set of techniques/theories governing the composition of a theatrical text.
>
> Theatrical Text: This is no longer meant to indicate the dramatic, literary text but rather the text of the theatrical performance (testo spettacolare), the performance text. This is conceived of as a complex network of different types of signs, expressive means, or actions, coming back to the etymology of the word "text" which implies the idea of texture, of something woven together.
>
> Dramaturgy can now be defined as the techniques/theory governing the composition of the performance-as-text (testo spettacolare); it is: the set of techniques/theories governing the composition of signs/expressive means/actions which are woven together to create the texture of the performance, the performance text.[22]

In De Marinis's theory, the audience is both the object of the performance, its target, and the receiver, or active interpreter of the performance. This refers to the "various receptive operations/actions the audience carries out:

20. Carlson, "Theatre Audiences and the Reading of the Performance," 83.

21. Marco De Marinis, "Dramaturgy of the Spectator," *Drama Review* 31, no. 2 (Summer 1987): 100–114. De Marinis's adaptation of the model reader to the model spectator is rooted in Umberto Eco, *The Role of the Reader* (Bloomington: Indiana University Press, 1979).

22. De Marinis, "Dramaturgy of the Spectator," 100.

perception, interpretation, aesthetic appreciation, memorization, emotive and intellectual response, etc."[23] It is only through these actions, observes De Marinis, that the performance is fully realized. For our purposes, two key concepts from De Marinis's work are important to explore: the model spectator and the structuring of the audience's attention. These concepts serve to remind us that the action of the spectators is not a mechanical process predetermined by the generators of the performance-text, but one of relative independence and autonomy working with the composition of the performance,

> occasionally adjusting each other's boundaries. Through its actions, by putting to work a range of definite semiotic strategies, the performance seeks to induce in each spectator a range of definite transformations, both intellectual (cognitive) and affective (ideas, beliefs, emotions, fantasies, values, etc.). The performance may even urge its audience to adopt particular forms of behavior such as in political theatre.[24]

The Model Spectator

Based on Eco's model reader, the model spectator, an implied receiver, is a hypothetical construct. "The idea is not to see the receptive processes of the empirical receiver as being rigidly present, not to indicate a normative reading that is somehow optimal, relevant, or correct, and to which every real receiver should try to conform."[25] De Marinis's model spectator, like Eco's model reader, is meant to remind us that production and reception are mutually linked. De Marinis's objectives for positing the model spectator are essentially the same as Eco's:

1. to show that production and reception of the performance, even given their reciprocal, partial autonomy, are closely connected;

23. Ibid., 101.
24. Ibid.
25. Ibid., 102.

2. to show exactly in what way and to what degree a performance anticipates a certain type of spectator (a certain type of reception); that is, to show precisely in what way and to what degree a performance tries to construct/predetermine a certain type of reception, both as part of its internal structure and as it unfolds.[26]

Closed and Open Performances

As a way of considering these problems, De Marinis follows Eco's lead, extending the concepts of closed and open texts to performances. For our purposes, these are still viable notions to consider, as we know that the scribes were writing and presenting the prophetic texts to a highly defined group of spectators.

Closed performances anticipate a "precise receiver and demand well-defined types of competence (encyclopedic, ideological, etc.) for their 'correct' reception."[27] The success of these performances relies heavily on the real audience corresponding to the anticipated audience. When there is a transparent relationship between the real and the anticipated audience, it is also easier to assume the audience into the world of the drama and make them active participants. This is certainly the case in Amos's oracles against the foreign nations. Open performances, on the other hand, "make a point of addressing themselves to a receiver who is neither too precise, nor too clearly defined in terms of their encyclopedic, intertextual, or ideological competence."[28] Open performances leave plenty of room for interpretive freedom.

Structuring the Spectator's Attention

De Marinis points out several key factors that must be kept in mind when thinking about the relationship between performance and spectator, and in particular, getting and holding the spectator's attention. Spectators have selective attention and will shift their focus from location to location, object to object, depending on the kind and quality of the stimuli and their own interests. In the case of theatrical performance, writes De Marinis, "there is no doubt that the sensory faculties of the perceiving subject are called upon

26. Ibid., 103.
27. Ibid.
28. Ibid.

to sustain an effort, to which, for both quantity and quality, there is not equivalent in any other artistic field."[29] Though De Marinis is referring to the modern theatre with all of its elements (lighting, sound, scenic, costume), the fact remains that live performance, even in its simplest form, is *work* for the spectator. "Reading" the performance—by focusing, defocusing, and refocusing as the sounds, gestures, and movements of the actor bring an entirely new reality into existence—is an effort even if all the performance work is being done by a single scribal actor. "It is worth repeating that without this basic *decoupage* and selection carried out by their attention, the spectators would not be in a position to work out their own 'reading' strategies for the performance, nor to give it first a local and then, gradually, a global meaning."[30] In order to facilitate this "reading," the performance-text, or what Beckerman would call the *act-scheme,* seeks to predispose and direct the spectator's attention through some kind of hierarchy of arrangement. De Marinis points out that such a hierarchy generally takes two forms:

> 1. As a stable hierarchy which, broadly speaking, conforms to "rules of genre," the most obvious example being the privileged status of the verbal text in the Western theatrical tradition.
>
> 2. As a shifting hierarchy where a whole range of focalizing and/or defocalizing devices operates within the one performance, a large portion of these devices being the scenic, lighting, and sound effects.[31]

Clearly, in the case of the scribe-as-actor's relationship to his spectators, we have a stable hierarchy; a stable hierarchy created scribes whose own selection and feedback processes brought about a performance-text *witnessed* primarily by spectators who were unable to read the text as literature.

29. Ibid., 107.
30. Ibid.
31. Ibid., 108.

Audience and Performance

A performance, writes Beckerman, "gives us something and nothing to respond to."[32] The *something* is people using their bodies, voices, and the world around them to make something appear for us. A performance is a gift and the gift is for someone: the audience, or spectators. In performance the audience is not only integral—it is essential. Remember: *Theatre and drama occur when another or others isolated in time and space present themselves to another or others.* The presence of the spectator is required. If there is no audience, there is no theatre or drama. The *something* a performance gives us, writes Beckerman, can be referred to as the iconic element of the performance: "the element offered to us for display."[33] Sound, color, movement—all of these are iconic elements heightened by the very fact that they are on display for spectators. "They are the something given."[34]

The *nothing* we respond to is the dialectic element. In Beckerman's words, it is "the air that crackles from the interchange between one actor and another, between one moment and another."[35] It is the interplay between the place of presentation, the presenters, and the spectators. It is a give-and-take that requires both the actor and the spectator as participants:

> Initially, the give-and-take occurs between the physical activity of presentation and the sensitized organs of perception in an audience. Gradually the sensory response expands into the imaginative. Entertainment is thus a precondition to other specific responses. Something must be held between the presenter and the receiver. Such and such an action, being entertained, should effect entertainment in the audience.[36]

Beckerman is here describing that which occurs in the drama. The sensory response to the iconic, that which can be seen and heard, expands into the

32. Bernard Beckerman, *Theatrical Presentation: Performer, Audience, and Act* (ed. Gloria Brim Beckerman and William Coco; New York: Routledge, 1990), 73.

33. Ibid.

34. Ibid.

35. Ibid., 74.

36. Beckerman, *Dynamics of Drama: Theory and Method of Analysis* (New York: Drama Book Specialists, 1979), 145.

imaginative response of the dialectic, that which is created when the actor assumes the life of the character and the audience engages in the imaginative interplay along with the actor. Another way of putting this is to describe what the audience does as participating in the willing suspension of disbelief.[37] "The audience entertains a dynamic illusion of life. This illusion has a virtual existence: a life of its own according to its own organic nature. . . . But the illusion is also a reflection; it mirrors actual human situations. We see through the action to actuality."[38] In the history of the literary theatre, the balance between the illusion and actuality changes dramatically from historical period to historical period. In fact, the balance changes considerably within each historical period depending on the form the drama takes. For example, in the allegorical dramas of the medieval world, much like Greek tragedy, events are highly compressed and function as analogues for the larger events of life. The audience relies on a transparency between the drama and the experience of their own lives. The performance facilitates the spectators' ability to see through the enacted event to the core of its meaning. They willingly suspend their disbelief ("I know that is John Doe playing Everyman") because of the simultaneous belief that the drama is illuminating another reality. "There is the tug of the play, urging us to submerge ourselves fully in its life. There is the restraint of the larger world. In agreeing to believe the fiction, we invoke an unspoken convention that such belief is privileged."[39] In essence, we participate in a three-way communication process that can be visualized in the following way:

37. The "willing suspension of disbelief" has become a phrase of common usage. Samuel Taylor Coleridge coined the phrase in the nineteenth century. Though Coleridge was referring to a reader's response to poetry, the phrase has since summarized most of the human experience to art. It has also been used extensively to describe the audience's dual relationship to the drama. Though an audience knows the actor is engaged in the creation of an illusory world, we enter that world in search of both reality and truth.

38. Beckerman, *Dynamics of Drama,* 146.

39. Ibid., 133.

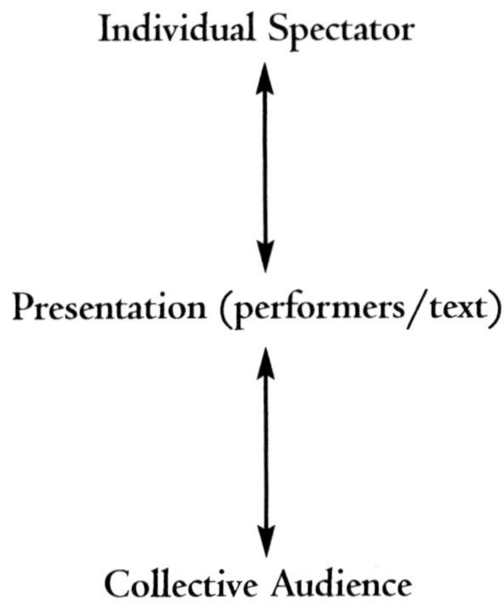

In the case of the prophetic drama, what we are calling the performative world (the prophetic text) has a transparent relationship to the real world (the actual lives of the scribe's audience). In other words, the scribe's audience, though removed from the actual prophet's audience by time, could clearly see through the illusory world of the drama to the actual world of their own relationship to God.

> The drama stands for all of life. As such, it must abstract from experience more than other forms of expression. It also exists only in communal interplay and, therefore, must achieve a high level of generalization. While the abstraction and generalization may look backward to its sources—the specific instances and actual observations of life—they also look forward toward formal realization. Through the processes of selection and feedback, actuality is refined into a "pure" analogue of a larger reality.[40]

The text, or script of the drama, is the result of ongoing interaction between content and presentational structures, or between what is to be performed and how it is to be performed. Is the performance to involve props, music, dance, changes in voice, patterned gesture? Historically, this interaction is governed by a selection and feedback process whereby audiences affect both the content and presentational structures by expressing their

40. Ibid., 147.

pleasure or displeasure. When something fails in performance, everyone knows it (playwright, actors, and audience). However, the interaction between content and performance structures also shapes audience response. It is a symbiotic relationship that occurs as a result of the live interchange between actors, act, and audience.

> First of all, it appears that there is a dynamic give and take between theatrical form and extra-theatrical materials.[41] On the one hand, with the earliest Greek tragedies we see that a general structural pattern has evolved, obliging playwrights to assimilate any new material into that established pattern. Yet in another instance, we see that the [medieval] church has accepted specific episodes for transmutation from biblical to dramatic form although the form itself is not yet fully developed. These two different relationships between content and structure should warn us that there is a continuous process of accepting and rejecting materials for the stage.[42]

However, Beckerman observes, most ongoing theatrical systems are made up of "accepted" presentational structures that can absorb new material for lengthy periods of time. "The accepted forms are not necessarily rigid; rather they emerge as historical models which a society demands of performers and playwrights. It may do so through the natural response of the audience. Or it may act more coercively, as when the Athenians forbade Phrynichus ever to deal with contemporary subject matter."[43] Either way, content, shape, and form of the presentation is inextricably linked with audience response.

In very general terms, Beckerman divides audiences into two types: random and communal.[44] These are useful categories because, between them, they cover the range of audiences we can imagine on the continuum between those who were witness to the prophets themselves, those who were witness to the growing oral tradition, and those who were witness to the scribal tradition. As we move toward the audiences of the scribal tradition, we move toward a more

---

41. "Extra-theatrical materials" can include events from daily existence, reference to art objects or images, objects of common use, etc.

42. Beckerman, *Theatrical Presentation*, 76.

43. Ibid.

44. Beckerman, *Dynamics of Drama*, 135.

highly developed communal audience.

Random Audience

Street theatre performances are good places to find random audiences: those individuals who select to stay and watch something when it starts happening. We can imagine that this was true for many of the prophets, who had to find a way to get people's attention and then get them to stay and listen. They are not really completely random, as the reasons for staying to watch and listen generally tend to assemble the group based on some similar outlook, such as intellectual appeal, economic factors, or human curiosity.

Communal Audience

At its most fully formed, writes Beckerman, a communal audience "consists of people whose total social experience is at one with each other and the presenters."[45] In the fully formed communal audience, the values, language, and thoughts of all involved in the theatrical experience are identical, or as close to identical as possible (De Marinis's *closed performance*). This kind of community makes multiple communication possible. The presenter's voice meets with less resistance, and the shared identity between presenter and audience is reaffirmed through performance. However, as Beckerman points out, communal pressure also imposes restrictions on the substance and content of presentations as well as the methods of presentation. A common ground must be established between presenter, presentation, and spectator. This figure-ground relationship, as Beckerman names it, brings together the world of the drama, the background circumstances, and the audience sensibilities. When a drama is first constructed, as is the case with the prophetic drama, the world of the action "is usually the world of the audience—either the actual physical world or, more likely and essentially, the social, psychological, and moral world."[46] And since the dramatic text does not have time to create a world of its own, it relies on signs and symbols to create the world it presents to the spectators. "The audience fills in that world from its own experience if the signs and symbols excite its sensibility. . . . This psychological ground, linking audience world and playworld, then supports the particular

45. Ibid.
46. Ibid., 139.

response aroused by artistically shaped action."[47]

We suggest that as the prophetic tradition moved from the actual prophets, through an oral tradition, to the written scribal tradition, there was a transition from a random to a communal audience.

Prophetic Tradition	**Scribal Tradition**
→	→
Random Audience	**Communal Audience**

For example, Amos the prophet, in addition to the difficulties associated with heeding God's call, had the additional problem of generating his own audience. In the role of prophet-actor, Amos not only generated his own performance-text, but he had to find and convince people to listen to him. But in the case of the scribe-as-Amos, a communal audience was already at the scribe's disposal. The fact that they were largely illiterate is really of very little consequence to the performed text of the scribe. Their ability to be audience to the performed-reading-of-text was influenced by their shared values and background, not by their ability to read the written word. This shift in audience and their likely receptivity to the performed-text of the scribe represents another dimension of the power the scribe appropriated from the prophet. The amount of resistance a prophet would experience with his audience would be much greater than the resistance faced by the scribe.[48] In the case of Amos's oracles against foreign nations, Amos, the foreigner, faced disbelief, rejection, and possibly violence. The scribe who enacts Amos can use the imagined resistance and rejection as part of his virtual existence, but faces none of it personally. In fact, what the scribe-as-actor gains from enacting Amos for a communal audience is the power of the presence of God in the final oracle against Israel.

The audience's relationship to the background of the action is critical

47. Ibid.

48. See the discussion in chapter 3 on projects and resistance, pages 80–83.

to our understanding of the performative nature of the prophetic text. Historically speaking, dramatic texts display one of two tendencies: The background represents communal values shared and confirmed by the creator of the text, or the background represents values the action of the drama seeks to directly or indirectly attack. "In every play, the writer presumes a background which he shocks [attacks] or reconfirms. Schematically speaking, we can say that dramatic action plays off the backboard of social and psychological values and customs, which, even if sketched in lightly or merely assumed, are always present."[49]

AMOS: A PERFORMANCE PROPHET

Having established a number of important concepts that make up an emerging methodology, performance criticism, we will now apply performance criticism to the book of Amos. Why Amos? Is there some special reason why our focus should now be limited only to this one biblical book? A partial answer to these questions is provided by David Peterson: "Amos and the scholarship devoted to it offer a microcosm of work on prophetic literature. Virtually every method or perspective available has been exercised on these nine chapters."[50] The great amount of scholarly literature on Amos provides a rich stockpile of information and examples of research that in many ways exemplify the work done on all the rest of the Hebrew prophetic books.[51] And so, from that perspective, Amos is a logical choice to test the application of a novel method of criticism. Moreover, all of the work expended on Amos has made the prophet and the literature bearing his name accessible and familiar. We can rely upon the work of other, fine scholars, understanding, in so doing, that many of the textual and historical difficulties have been addressed by others. We are thereby free to focus on the specifics of performance criticism.

The structure of the book of Amos has drawn considerable attention

---

49. Beckerman, *Dynamics in Drama*, 141.

50. David Peterson, "The Book of the Twelve / The Minor Prophets," in *The Hebrew Bible Today: An Introduction to Critical Issues* (ed. S. L. McKenzie and M. Graham; Louisville, Ky.: Westminster John Knox, 1998), 107.

51. See, for instance, the extensive bibliographies in the following: Gerhard Hasel, *Understanding the Book of Amos* (Grand Rapids: Eerdmans, 1991); Henry Thompson, *The Book of Amos: An Annotated Bibliography* (Lanham, Md.: Scarecrow, 1997); Roy Melugin, "Amos in Recent Research," *Currents in Research:Biblical Studies* 6 (1998): 65–101; and Carroll R., *Amos.*

from the scholarly community. Several scholars, and the number seems to be growing, have closely examined the complicated literary patterns resident in the document and have commented on the rhetorical value of those patterns and structures. David Dorsey has highlighted the series of heptads and chiasms in the book that lend beauty and elegance to the structure of the book as it now stands.[52] Maynet and Bovati have also noticed the chiastic structures in the book and coined the term *rhetorique biblique* to describe the concentric structures and repetitions that hold the document together.[53] Common to these examinations of the book is an appreciation for the response of either the listening or reading audience to the patterns and structures found in the document.[54]

There are several compositional theories of the book of Amos that implicitly assume a performative aspect to the prophet's work. That prophetic performance, in one fashion or another, has been thought to have influenced the structure of the Amos document. Karl Moller has considered the performative aspects of the book of Amos in the "presentation of the prophet in debate."[55] The book, Moller contends, is a debate, of sorts, between the prophet and his audience, the debate becoming a rhetorical device used by the scribal editors of the book.[56] This "debate as rhetorical device," Moller goes on to say, is not unique to Amos but can be identified in Hosea as well, and so may, with benefit, be applied to more than just

52. See David Dorsey, "Literary Architecture and Aural Structuring Techniques in Amos," *Biblica* 73 (1992): 305–30.

53. See Pietro Bovati and Roland Maynet, *Le livre du prophete Amos* (Rhetorique biblique 3; Paris: Cerf, 1994); and Roland Meynet, *Rhetorical Analysis: An Introduction to Biblical Rhetoric* (Sheffield: Sheffield Academic Press, 1998).

54. See also, for example, Hans Walter Wolff's discussion of Amos 3:3–8. Wolff imagines this text as a justification of the prophet to a disinclined audience. Hans Walter Wolff, *Joel and Amos* (Hermenia; Philadelphia: Fortress Press, 1977), 184. James Linville makes a similar observation when describing Amos "justifying himself to hecklers in his audience." Linville, "'Amos among the Dead Prophet's Society': Re-reading the Lion's Roar," *Journal for the Study of the Old Testament* 90 (2000): 64.

55. Karl Moller, "'Hear This Word against You': A Fresh Look at the Arrangement and Rhetorical Strategy of the Book of Amos," *Vetus Testamentum* 50 (2000): 510.

56. Ibid., 511. Moller believes that Wolff, too, although using different terminology, has identified the "dialogical dimension of the text" (509). According to Moller, it is the editors or redactors who "present us with the debate between Amos and his eighth-century audience" (509). In other words, the scribe of the book of Amos has made both Amos and the eighth-century audience characters in his literary rendition.

one example of prophetic literature.[57]

Moller makes another observation that is important for our discussion. In a performance, the actor is not the only one present. An audience is assumed, and that audience has an important role to play. Moller makes his point as follows:

> I want to ask, that is to say, whether the reflection of the debate, which I have deemed to have discovered in the book, might not be the result of there being sketches of the prophet's public appearances, sketches that not only preserve Amos' words but also give us, by way of implication, some of the ideas of the audience's reaction.[58]

The performative mode of thought ("sketches of the prophet's public appearances") that involves implicit activity and gives some indication of the presence of audience can be discernable in the Amos document. And these descriptions are central to Moller's perception of the structure of the book: "While the notion of a debating prophet is not a new one, my claim that the book of Amos *captures* or *presents* the debate between Amos and his original audience and utilizes it as a rhetorical means of persuasion is different from traditional redaction-critical readings."[59]

Performance criticism is not the same as redaction criticism, narrative criticism, or form criticism, but stands alongside these time-honored methodologies applied to the biblical text. In some ways, performance criticism uses insights from these other forms of criticism and combines them with an appreciation for audience response in order to present the dynamics present in a social event, namely, performance.

Gerhard Pfeifer is another scholar who has investigated the interplay between presenter and audience in the book of Amos. Pfeifer argues for the authenticity of the various sections of the book of Amos based upon his consideration of the rhetoric and theology that, for him, tie the book together. His method considers the book as a complicated dance revolving around the descriptions of the acts and character of Yahweh.[60] In the book,

57. Ibid., 507.

58. Ibid.

59. Ibid., 512.

both prophet and audience are brought to the swaying rhythms of the poetic dance.

The implicit qualities of the prophetic presentation in the book of Amos have not escaped unnoticed. James Linville has written on what he considers the "polysemy" of the book, that is, the ambiguities and subtleties that are intended within the text.[61] An integral part of his presentation of Amos is what Linville refers to as a "textual" audience: "One of the premises of this paper is widely accepted: that the rhetorical strategy guiding at least part of the book depends upon a response from the audience."[62] The polysemy or subtleties in the book form the "implicit" material that is to be expected in the formation of script. In fact, Linville comes very close to describing a virtual or performative space and time. He suggests that "perhaps the absence of many details only makes the reader's imagination work harder, to build a world *for* Amos, and so all the easier to enter it oneself."[63]

If, as many recent commentators indicate, the prophecy of Amos began as a prophetic performance that was subsequently transformed into a written medium, a word must be said concerning the formation of the book of Amos. It has become commonplace to recognize that the book of Amos is the result of several stages of composition and editorial activity. Perhaps the most extensively developed examinations of the stages of composition applied to the book of Amos have been presented by Hans Walter Wolff in his commentary on Joel and Amos and by Dirk Rottzoll in an edited publication of his doctoral dissertation.[64] Wolff identifies six distinct compositional layers beginning in the eighth century and concluding in the postexilic era. Others have identified stages of composition, yet not the same ones as Wolff.[65] The repeated "re-presentation" of the prophet in the literary tradition deserves our attention. For our purposes, these stages of composi-

---

60. Gerhard Pfeifer, "Die Fremdvölkersprüche des Amos—spatäre vaticinia ex eventu?" *Vetus Testamentum* 38 (1988): 230–33.

61. See James Linville, "Visions and Voices: Amos 7–9," *Biblica* 80 (1999): 22–42; and Linville, "Amos among the Dead Prophet's Society."

62. Linville, "Amos among the Dead Prophet's Society," 62

63. Ibid.

64. See Hans Walter Wolff, *Joel and Amos* (trans. Waldemar Janzen, S. Dean McBride, and Charles Muenchow; Hermeneia; Philadelphia: Fortress, 1977); and Dirk Rottzoll, *Studien zur Redaction und Komposition des Amosbuches* (Berlin: De Gruyter, 1996).

65. See Coote, *Amos among the Prophets*; and Alberto J. Soggin, *The Prophet Amos: A Translation and Commentary* (trans. J. Bowden; London: SCM Press, 1987).

tion can be considered performances involving an interaction between scribe and audience. Coote suggests as much: "Each stage of recomposition represents an interpretation of Amos' words, and thus an actualization of them, a reading and understanding of them *that makes them real and important in a new and different present.*[66]

The process of literary representation of the prophetic event introduces a second level of performance. The scribe, as it were, usurps the performance from the prophet and makes the prophet a character in his new version of the prophetic drama. The scribal performance can be structured in the brief outline below:

Amos: An Outline

I. Introduction (1:1)
II. Oracles (1:2–6:14)
   a. Oracles against nations (1:2–2:16)
   b. Words of the prophet (chs. 3–6)
      1. Divine response (3:1–11)
      2. Judgment (3:13–4:13)
      3. Funerary dirge (5:1–17)
      4. Day of the Lord (5:18–27)
      5. Indictments on immorality (6:1–14)
III. Visions (7:1–9:15)
   a. Visions (7:1–9; 8:1–9:15)
   b. Amos narrative (7:10–17)

Our application of performance criticism to the book of Amos dips into each of the main sections of the "scribal performance." In the next two chapters, we will apply performance criticism to the oracles against the nations, to selections from the words of the prophet, and to selections taken from the visions.

66. Coote, *Amos among the Prophets*, 3 (italics ours).

CHAPTER FIVE

The Amos Oracles

In this chapter, we explore how performance criticism and the performance mode of thought can be readily applied to the first part of the book of Amos. As hinted at in the opening verses, the book is divided into two large sections: oracles and visions. Here we will make application to a selection of the oracles. In the next chapter, we will consider a performance criticism of the visions.

Amos 1:3–2:16 consists of a series of oracles against foreign nations followed by a judgment oracle against Israel.[1] These speeches provide the first and easily observable instance of orality in the Amos document.

PERFORMANCE ARENA

Carol Fontaine has written a fascinating book with concerns related to the main focus of our work here. Fontaine argues that some of the sayings in the book of Proverbs functioned as performative material that was dramatized by

1. Excellent critical work has been done on Amos. Several of the leading commentaries, with thorough references to the scholarly literature, are: Hans Walter Wolff, *Joel and Amos* (Philadelphia: Fortress, 1977); Shalom Paul, *Amos* (Minneapolis: Fortress, 1991); and John Hayes, *Amos, the Eighth-Century Prophet: His Time and His Preaching* (Nashville: Abingdon, 1988).

women in ancient Israel.[2] While recognizing that we are dealing with different sets of data—Fontaine with Proverbs and we with the Prophets—our interests, nevertheless, are very similar in that we are looking to contextualize pieces of the literature of the Old Testament in a performative setting. Part of Fontaine's argument is dependent upon the theoretical construction of a performance arena. She identifies a performance arena as

> a special location, spatial, temporal or interpersonal, where oral performance occurs and a unit of folklore is invoked. It is the "compressed" nature of the folklore item, its "immanent referentiality," that accounts for its ability to call up a world of meanings, referencing a portion of a culture's thought world through employment of a compact linguistic medium.[3]

This arena is recognizable, and in fact the characteristics of the arena serve to "cue" the performer and audience that a performance is about to take place. Fontaine cites Richard Bauman and his work in establishing a set of characteristics, some of which can be transferred to literature in which a performance is embedded.[4] These characteristics include: appeal to tradition, disclaimers of performance, special codes or formulae, figurative language and paralinguistic features (e.g., gestures, pauses, movement). Fontaine uses the following characteristics to identify entrance to a performance arena in which the proverbs played and that can still be identified in the literary record:

1. *Introductory elements.* The proverb is prefaced by an appeal to tradition in which both parties of the conversation or performance give implicit recognition to the value of the traditional saying to follow. For example, a proverb can be introduced by "As it is said," or some similar introductory phrase.

2. *Out-of-context intrusion of figurative language in the use of the proverb.* Fontaine

2. See Carole Fontaine, *Smooth Words: Women, Proverbs, and Performance in Biblical Wisdom* (London: Sheffield Academic Press, 2002).

3. Ibid., 158.

4. Ibid., 163. See Richard Bauman, *Verbal Art as Performance* (Prospect Heights, Ill.: Waveland, 1977), 8–22.

makes the point that effective performative use requires that "users and hearers, locked in conflict or ambiguity, come together in temporary unity as the exchange proceeds: both share a fluency in their culture's body of proverbs, and both are linked in the moment of the citation."[5] That is, a proverb is inserted in a conversation or a dialogue to make a point that becomes clear to all participants by the presence of the proverb. The value of the proverb is dependent upon both parties agreeing to enter into a created reality in which the metaphor of the proverb is real and effective.

3. *Linguistic features.* The proverbs are recognizable by their shared and typical linguistic features (brevity, rhyme, alliteration, parallelism). They have a recognizable form that sets them apart from nontypical forms of human dialogue. That is, the proverb is in recognizable form. That recognizable form alone cues the hearer or reader into a range of interpretive options that are not present without the recognition of that form.[6]

The same characteristics can be identified at work with the oracles of Amos:

1. Introductory elements. The prophetic oracles typically have an introductory phrase that functions as marking off the following oracle from the surrounding literature or presumed speech. "Thus says the LORD" or some variant is common fare in the prophetic dialogue.

2. Out-of-context intrusion of figurative language. In the prophetic performance, a created reality is also invoked. Both the prophet and the audience interact to create a reality in which the unseen is seen and the symbolic becomes efficacious. The created reality of the prophet allows the certainty of the oracle for the prophet and the power of the oracle for the audience.

5. Fontaine, *Smooth Words*, 165.
6. Ibid., 165–66.

3. *Linguistic features.* Prophetic oracles also retain a number of recognizable linguistic characteristics. Whether they are messenger speeches, judgment oracles, or oracles against nations, there is ample evidence that at least some of the prophetic oracles are in recognizable form. Prophetic vision displays, too, may have a recognizable form so that observers, even without hearing the actual words or seeing the specific actions, may be able to conclude that a prophetic event was taking place. This is clearly the case in chapter 7 of Amos. Amaziah is able to include Amos among the prophets (or, in his words, *seer*) simply because he perceived Amos as doing something that is the proper behavior of the prophets he knew so well.

Our effort shall now be to see how well this "performance arena" manifests itself in the oracles of the prophet from Tekoa.[7]

ORACLES AGAINST THE FOREIGN NATIONS (1:3–2:6)

Shalom Paul has demonstrated the literary connectedness of the oracles against the foreign nations through the presence of a concatenous (chain link) literary pattern.[8] Despite this literary weaving, the oracle against Judah (2:4–5) is thought by some to have originated from a different editorial period due to a change in terminology and stylistic variations. Paul, however, has provided ample evidence to argue for the authenticity of this oracle and its integral connectedness to those that precede it.[9] With the conclusion to the

7. There have been previous examinations of the oracles in Amos as examples of liturgical, royal court, or clan wisdom performances. Our concern is not so much to place the performance within the context of one social location (e.g., cult, royal court, wisdom tradition) but to examine the performance itself. See Ernst Wurthein, "Amos-Studien," *Zeitschrift für die alttestamentliche Wissenschaft* 62 (1949–1950): 10–52; Graf Reventlow, *Das Amt des Propheten bei Amos* (Göttingen: Vandenhoeck & Ruprecht, 1962); and Walter Brueggemann, "Amos iv 4–13 and Israel's Covenant Worship," *Vetus Testamentum* 15 (1965): 1–15. An alternate view was put forward by S. Terrien that placed the prophet within the context of the wisdom circles. See Terrien, "Amos and Wisdom," in *Israel's Prophetic Heritage* (ed. B. W. Anderson and W. Harrelson; New York: Harper, 1962), 108–15; William McKane, *Prophets and Wise Men* (London: SCM Press, 1965); and Hans Walter Wolff, *Amos the Prophet: The Man and His Background* (trans. F. McCurley; Philadelphia: Fortress, 1973).

8. Paul, *Amos,* 11ff. See also Shalom Paul, "Amos 1:3–2:3: A Concatenous Literary Pattern," *Journal of Biblical Literature* 40 (1971): 397–403.

9. Paul, *Amos,* 21–27.

oracle against Judah, the prophet is prepared to turn his attention to the Israelite audience (2:6–16).

If we look at the oracles against the foreign nations in terms of their inherent dramatic structure, an inner life is revealed that teems with the presence of the prophet/performer as well as the variation of increasing and decreasing intensity necessary to facilitate dramatic activity. The pattern of dramatic activity resonates with the idea of a concatenous literary pattern, or linked series of episodes. In the structure of dramatic activity, segments are linked together in a variety of ways—either by the performative devices the "actor" brings to the structure, the literary devices that are established by tradition, or by a combination of both. Following the same pattern we applied to the example of I Samuel, we will look at Amos's oracles against foreign nations from the following framework:

- Precipitating context
- Explicit and implicit activity
- Project
- Crux

Precipitating Context

Since the oracles against foreign nations begin almost immediately in the book of Amos, it is necessary to turn to the historical context of the text in order to establish the precipitating context for the dramatic activity. Essentially, the precipitating context is the information supplied before a segment of dramatic activity begins. Sometimes this information arises solely from the performer himself/herself, sometimes from the source of the drama (myth, legend, folklore, history), and as the drama progresses, from preceding segments. In our case, the precipitating context is well defined in the introduction to the book: "The words of Amos, who was among the shepherds of Tekoa, which he saw concerning Israel in the days of King Uzziah of Judah and in the days of King Jeroboam son of Joash of Israel, two years before the earthquake" (1:1).

The correlation of the two monarchs, one of Judah and one of Israel, places the prophetic event somewhere between 760 and 750 B.C.E. Some have described this as Israel's golden age, a period of territorial expansion and national prosperity. Under Jeroboam II, peace with the Arameans was won and land repossessed, expanding the reach of the nation almost to the extent enjoyed under the, by now, mythic reigns of David and Solomon. Excavations conducted on major urban sites of Israel such as Samaria, Hazor, Megiddo, and Dan illustrate the material benefits of this peace and prosperity. Yet the national wealth does not seem to have been shared by all. The unequaled prosperity of the elite was matched by a growing disenfranchisement of the poor. The Amos prophecies themselves describe an economic climate that favored the few at the expense of the many (2:6–8 and 6:4–6). The golden façade covered a social unease experienced by those destined to live in the anonymous underbelly of the northern nation.

Something else was taking place in the decade between 760 and 750 B.C.E. The mighty Assyrian Empire was beginning to stir. By the end of Jeroboam's reign the Assyrian shadow would lie heavily upon the Levant and people would tremble by a different kind of quaking in the ground, one caused by the pounding feet of the Assyrian armies.

For the initial audience, however, much more specificity is allowed than the simple correlation of two kings. The writer of this introduction recalls a major event, one that everyone must have been able to recall—an earthquake—and places the Amos performance exactly two years earlier. There is little doubt that recalling for the audience the horrific memory of the shaking and trembling of the very earth under their feet provided the exact backdrop that the scribal performer wanted for the announcement of the roaring of the Lord. This then sets the stage or provides the precipitating context for the oracles that follow.

Explicit and Implicit Activity

We are treating the oracles against foreign nations as a single dramatic segment, with each oracle nesting within the whole and creating a pattern of increasing and decreasing activity that ultimately leads to the judgment oracle against Israel. In fact, it is from the oracles themselves that the precipitating context emerges. By the time we get to the oracle against Israel, Amos, who speaks as the Lord in the oracles against foreign nations, has established the pattern of transgressions Israel is to be held accountable for. It is important to remember that this information emerges as "spoken," as delivered by the prophet. In other words, the precipitating context is performed. Not only is it performed, but the *how* of the performance is established right from the beginning: "The LORD roars from Zion" (1:2). As we turn to the explicit and implicit nature of the activity of the oracles, the image of the Lord as roaring lion is a critical stage direction. It establishes a high level of intensity for the delivery of the oracles. In terms of the performative context for the prophet, particularly as he moves from "Thus says the LORD," to speaking as the Lord ("I will not revoke . . ."), the roaring lion is a very useful image. The explicit activity of the oracles against foreign nations is clear and distinct, establishing a rhythmic pattern of exchange between the prophet and his spectators. Each oracle contains its own crux, or moment of highest intensity, as well as its own decrescence, or movement away from that intensity, punctuated by a concluding phrase: "says the LORD." The two frames of each oracle—the opening, "Thus says the LORD," and the concluding, "says the LORD," are perhaps the most significant in terms of explicit and implicit activity because they represent moments of transformation for the prophet. Each "Thus says the LORD" signifies the moment of transformation from Amos the prophet to Amos as the Lord. The concluding "says the LORD" reverses the transformation, allowing the resumption of Amos the prophet. The prophet himself becomes the link between the real world and the performance world. The prophet becomes the performance personified.[10]

Amos as prophet ⟶ Amos/as the Lord ⟶ Amos as prophet

Each oracle is bound by the time and space of Amos's presentation. In other words, it is Amos himself who "sets the stage" by proclaiming, "The LORD roars from Zion, and utters his voice from Jerusalem." This performative moment, spoken to get the attention of his audience, alerts the spectators that a transformation is about to occur. In the culture of prophetic performance, spectators are brought into the time and space of the drama that is about to be played out in front of them. It is now possible for Amos to move between prophet and the Lord by employing the appropriate devices ("Thus says the LORD," "says the LORD"), which have become part of the specta-

10. David Stacey observes, "The prophet was *himself* a symbol." Stacey, *Prophetic Drama in the Old Testament* (London: Epworth, 1990), 61.

tors' experience. For us, as twenty-first-century spectators, it is the moment of the house lights going down in a theatre, or the appearance of the first actor on the stage that suddenly alerts us to the beginning of the performance. Our awareness and attention shift to the presence of the actor, and we have already begun our transition from the actual world of our everyday reality into the virtual world of the drama we have come to see. Our transition is a combination of the work of the actor and the theatrical conventions and devices we are accustomed to.

Put yourself in the place of Amos. Imagine yourself, an outsider from uncertain economic standing and questionable political ties, standing before a crowd of people who, at the very least, look upon you suspiciously, if not with disdain. You know that the purpose of your oracles against the foreign nations is merely a set-up for an oracle against the very people who have gathered around you. You know in advance that when you speak as the Lord, you will offer indictments, punishments, a litany of things the Lord hates and despises, culminating in an indictment of the very people gathered around you. As you progress through the oracles, the resistance from the spectators may grow and turn violent. After all, you stand before them as a poor shepherd from the south prophesying against "they who trample the head of the poor into the dust of the earth, and push the afflicted out of the way" (2:7). Amos's tension level is high right from the beginning: "The LORD roars from Zion." Fulfilling the activity of the prophet (Amos's project) produces the theatrical tension. The path of this tension is the action: oracles against foreign nations leading up to the oracle against Israel. The flow of this action creates the inner life of the drama: the sensations and the experiences that pass between Amos and the spectators. As Amos moves through the mounting tension of presenting the oracles, the inherent linear intensification and relaxation pattern of the drama is revealed. Clearly, he must somehow gain and hold the attention of these spectators if his project has any chance of being fulfilled by the time he reaches the oracle against Israel.

Explicit Activity	Implicit Activity
Opening speech: "The LORD roars . . ."	Who are Amos's spectators? How many are there, and where are they gathered? How does Amos create the roar of the Lord's voice? Do all the spectators immediately pay attention? Is there discussion among them? Does Amos wait for their full attention?
Oracle against Damascus	Does Amos look directly at his spectators when he speaks, "Thus says the LORD"? How long does he pause before speaking as the Lord? How does his voice change from speaking as prophet to speaking as Lord? Who does Amos look at or where does he look when proclaiming what will happen to the gate bars of Damascus? Does he choose a group of spectators who are then transformed into the people of Damascus? Are the spectators pleased at this oracle? If so, how do they show it? What feedback do they give Amos? Does their response motivate Amos to roar again as the Lord? Or are the spectators skeptical of Amos as prophet? How does Amos transition from speaking as the Lord back to a prophet: "says the LORD"?
Oracle against Gaza	Does the prophet "roar" as the Lord a second time? Does he shift his focus among the spectators to bring Gaza into the space? Does he point toward Gaza, causing spectators to look in that direction? Does his voice increase in pitch and volume? What other tactics does the prophet use to increase the tension? Does he move closer to the spectators and then withdraw? Does he pause to look at the spectators so he can take in their response?
Oracles against Tyre, Edom, and the Ammonites	How does the prophet's approach to the spectators change with these three oracles? The oracles against Tyre and Edom are shorter. The prophet does not return to "says the LORD" until after the oracle against the Ammonites. How does he use the rhythm change? Is he building momentum? Does his body, through gesture, help to increase the intensity of the compiling effect of oracle after oracle? How does he use his voice to effect these shorter, intensified "roars" up through the end of the oracle against the Ammonites when the voice of the prophet returns with "says the LORD"?

Explicit Activity	Implicit Activity
Oracle against Moab	Does Amos pause after the last oracle before transitioning into the oracle against Moab with "Thus says the LORD"? Does his eye contact with the spectators increase as he comes closer and closer to the oracle against Judah? Is the "roar" of the Lord reaching peak intensity? Are the spectators beginning to anticipate an oracle against them? How does the prophet gauge their response to him? What else does he do to keep the spectators from disengaging with him? Knowing that he is moving on a trajectory toward the oracle against Israel, what does the prophet do to prevent his spectators from arriving at that point before he wants them to? How does he use his voice and body to keep them with him in the moment, focused on Moab?
Oracle against Judah	The oracle against Judah does not end with "says the LORD," but transitions right into "Thus says the LORD," for the oracle against Israel. How does this rhythmic device help the prophet control the attention of his spectators? How might the prophet use this as a transition? Does he intensify the pitch and volume of his delivery, preparing to reach the crux, or final climactic point, of these oracles when speaking of Israel's transgressions? How does he alter his physical relationship to the spectators so that he is positioned for the final oracle? Does he place himself among them, or draw further away from them? Does he look for an opportunity to stand above them and physically dominate them by being on a higher plane? Does he use his voice and body to draw the spectators to him so that the oracle against Israel can begin at a lower pitch, with almost whispered intensity? What does he look for in the faces of and bodies of the spectators as he lists each transgression: delivering entire communities, pursuing "his brother with the sword," ripping open pregnant women. How does he manipulate his voice to make these images real for his spectators? What signs do they give back to him to make the prophet adjust his voice/body?

THE ORACLE AGAINST ISRAEL (2:6–16)

Before looking at the explicit and implicit activity of the oracle against Israel, it will be useful to return to some of our earlier observations concerning orality in the text. Our understanding of the double nature of the prophet (Amos as prophet/prophet as voice of the Lord) and the potential overall effect of this shifting is deepened by seeing the connection between a linguistic mode of understanding the text and a performance mode of the understanding the text as script.

Indictments that point to Israelite social abuse and framed in the third person occupy verses 6–8. In utilizing a distant conceptual linguistic mode, these verses operate much as the oracles that were delivered to the foreign nations. This third person, distant address gives way, however, to a first and second person, immediate mode of discourse in verses 9–11. The change is pronounced. First, through the use of the emphatic אנכי in verses 9, 10, and 13 and in the repeated use of the second person pronominal suffixes, the language of distance gives way to the discourse of immediacy. Yet the informality of oral discourse is not adopted altogether. Verses 9–13 retain certain formal and traditional characteristics. The phrase "I brought you up from the land of Egypt" of verse 10 is repeated in 3:1, and the odd inverse in chronological sequence between the destruction of the Amorites and the flight from Egypt in verses 9–10 allow the formation of a literary inclusio that presents the Amorites at the beginning of verse 9 and the end of verse 10.

The whole literary unit is brought to an end with a return to language of distance, both spatially and chronologically, in verses 14–16. The first and second person of verses 9–13 have given way to a return to third person discourse, and the temporal immediacy required by the question posed in verse 11 is replaced by reference to the distant "in that day" of verse 16. When compared to characteristics appearing on the orality in text graph (see chapter 2), it is apparent that this part of Amos fits nicely in the upper right or third quadrant—the quadrant labeled *performative.*

The section comprised of verses 9–13 establishes an immediate *we-now-here* that lends a heightened sense of tension to the whole series of oracles. The *reporting* of events that characterizes the oracles of 1:3–2:8 gives way to an *unfolding* of events in 2:9–13, drawing the audience into the performance by demanding at least nominal involvement through the invited audience assent requested in the divine speech of 2:9–11. The tension is brought to a climactic conflict in verse 11 by the question designed to elicit a decision from the audience. That conflict is resolved and the tension decreased as the language of immediacy recedes and the language of distance and monologue once again dominates the conclusion of the series in verses 14–16. Having reached the crux of the oracles (vv. 9–13), a new path of tension is developed by moving to a mode of reporting on the consequences for what Israel has done (vv. 14–16). Once again, the language of reporting events, which began the whole series in chapter 1, is used in 2:15–16 to communicate the factuality and finality of the judgment determined by the Lord.

The movement from distant to immediate address and back again has a definite performative quality. Dialectic modes of performance are dominated by tension and resistance. Tension results from the inherent risk to the performer (the prophet, the Israelites), and resistance is what the performer needs to overcome. Disobeying or ignoring the word of the Lord is riddled with risk for both the prophet and the people of Israel. Tension, in theatrical and dramatic terms, translates directly into immediacy. It is the force that binds the performer, the act, and the spectator together. Tension increases and decreases through modulation of communicative strategies and attempts at overcoming resistance, as Beckerman explains:

> It is the focus of the risk that resides in the act. . . . In dialectic presentation, if there is a real question of control, the resistance has the distinct potentiality of defeating the performer. The tension between the will to do the act and the obstacle to its fulfillment is thus neatly calibrated so that when the performer prevails, there is not so much awe but release.[11]

Beckerman's basic framework for the nature of dialectic presentation contains an essential pattern through which the communicative strategies Oesterreicher enumerates can be seen to take the shape of theatrical presen-

11. Bernard Beckerman, *Dynamics of Drama: Theory and Method of Analysis* (New York: Drama Book Specialists, 1979), 57.

tation. In theatrical and dramatic terms, these are patterns of conflict, and the tension and resistance are created by a modulation of a variety of physical, social, and psychological relationships. In this context, if we look at the relationship between explicit and implicit activity in the oracle against Israel, we can see how the increasing and decreasing patterns of tension present in the oracles leading up to this oracle reach a crux that is rooted in the rising and falling action of the entire series. In other words, the oracles against the foreign nations function as a series of segments leading up to the oracle against Israel, where the prophet-as-performer fulfills his project.

In the case of Amos's oracles against foreign nations, the delivery of the oracles is our concern. Again, since we do not have a record, such as a recording or videotape of Amos himself delivering the oracles, we have to rely on what we know about the nature of dramatic activity combined with the knowledge that the scribal tradition resulted in "performances" that were meant to imaginatively engage spectators in the prophetic experience. Whatever shape an action (oracle, vision, prophecy, warning) assumes, it is always governed by the essential structure of the presentational situation.[12] As a reminder, the key elements of performative structure, as distinct from literary structure, are

- Interplay between audience attention and act of presentation
- Performer's project (focus of his energies)
- Tension (increasing and decreasing)
- Spatiotemporal transformation

From these key elements, shapes of action are created; a performance map emerges with tempo, stride, posture, vocal tone, pitch, and gesture that creates the essential structure of the performance. At the very least, we must assume that these shapes of action were part of the performance mode of thought of the scribe as he structured the oracles against foreign nations that lead up to the oracle against Israel. The degree to which they were based on actual descriptions of what Amos did, or a combination of the oral tradition of Amos along with patterns of prophetic behavior available to the scribe, is a question we clearly cannot answer. However, as is the case with I Sam 3, we

12. Ibid., 56.

know that Amos was indeed a prophet and that a repeatable/reusable pattern of prophetic activity was preserved beyond his time. In the example of Amos's oracles against foreign nations, the shape of the action culminates in the oracle against Israel. The prophet's project for this section of the book of Amos takes on a clearly delineated spatiotemporal existence between verses 1:3 and 2:16. He has taken an "ethical tour" of the region, enumerating the transgressions against the Lord, ending up in Israel.

Explicit Activity	Implicit Activity
Oracle against Israel The Lord's indictment: "Is it not indeed so, O people of Israel?"	Does Amos speak "Thus says the LORD," differently for this final oracle? How does his voice reveal or mask whose transgressions are next? Does he pause and scan the crowd with his eyes to make sure that all the spectators are with him? Does he breathe in their anticipation, taking his cue from the crowd gathered around him? Does he point or gesture at the crowd as he names Israel? How does he shift into the more distant mode of address in verses 6–8? Does he look toward the "past" by looking above or beyond the spectators? Does the roar of his voice soften, leaving room for the roar to grow in verses 9–11? Does he pause at the end of verse 8, knowing that he is nearing the final question or moment of reckoning for the spectators? Does the prophet move in the space that has been created by the shifting of the spectators? Does he use spectators when he references the poor, the afflicted, the innocent, needy, or just? How does he use his body and voice together when speaking, "Also I brought you up out of the land of Egypt," so that the immediacy and intimacy of the Lord's relationship to the spectators at hand is felt and experienced by the crowd? Does his voice soften to reveal the Lord's love for Israel in the description of what the Lord did for them? What is

Explicit Activity	Implicit Activity
Oracle against Israel The Lord's indictment: "Is it not indeed so, O people of Israel?"	the response Amos hopes for when he (speaking as the Lord) asks the crowd, "Is it not indeed so, O people of Israel?" How does he transition from that point to "says the LORD"? How does the prophet mange the shifts of verses 12–16, moving back into a distant mode of communication but taking his spectators through the moment of indictment to the consequences of being pressed down and of perishing no matter how swift they are?

Project

In terms of Amos's *project,* we must remember that in the drama, the project is the focal point of the performer and the character. The performer's energy is projected toward achieving the character's project. What does the performer need to do in order to make the spectator believe that what she/he is experiencing is the inner life of the character? "It is in such a way that the project is the concrete focal point of a character's energy," says Beckerman, "and it is the project that the performer enacts."[13] In this portion of the script of Amos, we have Amos the shepherd of Tekoa who becomes Amos the prophet, who then acts as the Lord, shifting between roles as he progresses from oracle to oracle. Clearly, the project of Amos the shepherd is to fulfill the role of prophet. As a classic example of the "Other," coming from the southern state of Judah to prophesy against the northern state of Israel, we can safely assume that Amos's energies are consciously concentrated to achieve a specific goal. Why else would he make this trip to the northern state of Israel where he knows he will not be welcome?

Here we have a completely different project than we saw in the I Samuel example, where Samuel's project is more diffuse. The script of Amos presents us with a prophet who is already standing before his audience warning them that the Lord roars from Zion. We are presented with a very active series of dramatic segments, alerting us to a highly motivated and intentional project.[14]

13. Beckerman, *Dynamics of Drama,* 71.

14. See *segments* in the glossary.

Active segments of drama point to confrontation and to rising tension from a clear, active project. As Beckerman explains:

> The project . . . encompasses all kinds of energies that human beings exert. Some people dream into the future. Others concentrate their energies consciously. At one extreme we have determined efforts to achieve a specific goal. At the other, generalized impulses. For the purposes of analysis, we should discriminate between the project, the concrete image of a character's energy, and the energy itself. That energy, or impelling force, can be conscious or unconscious, rational or irrational, defined or vague. For the energy as a totality, of whatever type, I shall use the term "motivation." When the energy is conscious and specific, I shall call it "intention."[15]

We can define Amos's intention to go to Israel to prophesy against the foreign nations as part of his larger motivation to fulfill his role as prophet of the Lord. It is through Amos's project that the shape and flow of the action occurs. Amos can only fulfill his project by meeting and working through the resistance of his spectators. This is why our efforts to construct the possible path of the implicit activity are so important. It is what we cannot see in the script of Amos that we must imagine. It is also what must have been, at least partially, imagined by the scribe and by those who would have read, or presented, Amos aloud. The rhythmic pattern of increasing and decreasing tension brought about by Amos's pursuit of his project and his management of the inherent resistance of his spectators (Israelites from the north) creates our glimpse into the inner life of this drama. Beckerman describes this pattern:

How such linear intensification is organized is another matter. Here variation enters. Though a segment proceeds largely through intensification, there must also be reduction of intensity since human beings respond in phases. An unremitting increase in intensity would only force an audience to react self-protectively by dropping its attention. Consequently, a theatrical segment must have a rhythmic character. Its pulsation must be organic, involv-

15. Beckerman, *Dynamics of Drama*, 71.

ing not so much a beginning, middle and end, but intensification and decrescence, that is, a falling of tension. In the act of turning a somersault, the portion leading to the somersault is the period of intensification; the portion where the performer walks off the wire and bows is the decrescent. The somersault is the crux of the act. In essence, this is the modular unit of all theatrical action.[16]

Each oracle, including the oracle against Israel, displays a precise "pulsation," or linear pattern of intensification and decrescence. Variations to that pattern even link some oracles together in a rhythmic pattern while clearly separating others. This rhythmic pattern is enhanced by variations in the transgressions against the Lord, but result in a consistent pattern of punishment by fire.

Between "Thus says the LORD" and "says the LORD," is the rising and falling action of each oracle. Once Amos speaks "Thus says the LORD," and transitions into performing the Lord, the virtual world is established. As he concludes each oracle and transitions back into prophet with "says the LORD," he returns the spectators to the world of their immediate reality. The metaphor of the Lord as roaring lion begins to take on very practical dimensions in terms of Amos's performance as prophet. The lion's roar can be a very dynamic form of expression. It could be a roar of warning, a roar of threat, a roar of attack, a sustained roar, a roar that grows in intensity, a short roar, a roar that comes from above, in front of, or behind you. In each of these cases, the roar would have a distinct beginning and end. It is not just the literary form of the oracle that we need to investigate, but the performative implications present in the script. In terms of the explicit and implicit activity of the oracles, and the dialectic exchange between the Lord, the prophet, and the spectators, we need to focus on four levels simultaneously:

- What is the explicit activity of the oracle?
- What is the implicit activity of the prophet?
- What is the implicit activity of the spectators?
- How might these levels of activity come together to form the whole of the experience of Amos's oracles against foreign nations?

16. Ibid., 51.

Explicitly, Amos delivers seven oracles with parallel structure. Each begins with "Thus says the LORD" and ends with "says the LORD." Each follows the path of "three transgressions . . . and for four," followed by the Lord's proclamation that he will not "revoke punishment." That, in turn, is followed by the punishment itself. These seven oracles against foreign nations form the precipitating context for the oracle against Israel. From a performance perspective, Amos moves between the characters of prophet and the Lord. He displays a double nature, a movement between characters that would require certain performance choices (tone of voice, volume manipulation, gesture, varying eye contact, pauses) dictated by his ultimate project (motivation and intention).

The implicit activity keeps us focused on the performative nature of the prophetic act. How might things have been done, how might they have been enacted, how might spectators have responded, what techniques and devices might the prophet have used to gain and hold attention and to move spectators to belief and/or action? Most importantly, what does the explicit activity of the script available to us from the scribal tradition suggest in terms of implicit activity?[17]

Crux

As we examine the relationship between the explicit and implicit activity, it is important to keep in mind what we know of the circumstances of the dramatic segments before us:

- Amos is the Other—a foreigner from the south.
- The golden age of Israel has placed the nation at its economic apex.
- As we discover in the vision sequence, Amos was ordered never to prophesy in the royal sanctuary again.

17. We raise this question in relationship to the kinds of prophetic practices that seem to have been purged from the written prophetic tradition: the wearing of hairy mantles, self-inflicted wounds, bathing in their own blood, or a host of other ritualistic behaviors evidently employed by prophets as attested to by biblical descriptions of practices in Israel and Judah as well as a multitude of extra-biblical witnesses to the customs found in neighboring countries.

- It is a time of great transgressions (breaking of treaties, carrying entire communities into exile, desecrating corpses, rejecting the laws of the Lord).
- As a shepherd, Amos stands before his spectators as one of the "poor."[18]

The potential for tension and conflict is high. The human activity of confrontation, accusation, and threat carried in each of Amos's oracles is intense and seems to gather speed as the oracles progress. The potential patterns of resistance (performer to performer, performer to spectator, performer to act, performer to social and psychological forces) create patterns of flux, where each moment is on the verge of becoming something else. Beckerman describes this state: "Derived from the Latin word *tensus,* meaning 'stretched,' tension suggests the invisible lines of force between two contrasting poles. These lines are determined by the nature of contact between project and resistance within the segment and between segment and audience within the theatrical experience."[19]

In the case of the oracles, we see a pattern of flux that gradually moves Amos closer and closer to his spectators. His ethical tour of the region ultimately leads him right to the people of Israel. However, this is where he ends and not where he begins. The oracle against Israel could not possibly be his starting place. As the "other," the unwanted outsider, it is logical to assume that had he started with the oracle against Israel he could not have sustained the interest and attention of his spectators. He first needed to get them to listen to him, to win them over somehow. This is the intention part of his project. In order to achieve his overall motivation, to get his spectators to hear the word of the Lord, he must somehow motivate them to listen. The risk that they will turn on him when he reaches the oracle against Israel is high. Why would those spectators stay and listen to an outsider claim to be speaking to them on behalf of the Lord? If Amos does not win them over with the oracles against foreign nations, his overall project is likely to fail. His success depends on his ability to become a credible prophet in the eyes of his

18. T. Giles, "A Note on the Vocation of Amos in 7:14," *Journal of Biblical Literature* 111 (Winter 1992): 690–92.

19. Beckerman, *Dynamics of Drama,* 48.

spectators. What this pattern presents to us is a highly *intensive* structure in terms of performance.

For this reason, it is a mistake only to imagine Amos's presence in this drama. The people of Israel gathered around him are important characters as well. They too must come alive for us as we imagine the explicit and implicit activity. Even if we are imagining the scribe reading Amos aloud, the spectators present to the scribe are transformed into Amos's audience. It is what happens *between* them that allows us to glimpse the inner life of the drama. The trajectory of Amos's project is aimed at the ultimate moment of confrontation, or crux, with his spectators when he says, "Is it not indeed so, O people of Israel?" Speaking as the Lord at this moment, Amos recedes from the drama, leaving the Lord and the people of Israel present for the moment of reckoning. As seen in the following quote, it is precisely this type of performative moment that Beckerman identifies as exemplifying an intensive structure.

> In the Aristotelian frame of reference man is confined both in space and time. Subject to overwhelming circumstances his initiative is limited to *how* he will act not *what* he will do. As the action progresses, his range of choice is increasingly reduced, and he discovers that it is so reduced. The Aristotelian ideal compresses man into a moment of time when he will undergo an extreme turn of fortune (*peripeteia*) at the very instant that he undergoes an extreme shift of realization (*anagnorisis*). Because this moment of time into which man has been forced results from progressive intensification of pressures upon him, let us refer to this type of structure as intensive.[20]

Intensive modes of dramatic structure are the products of specific causes. The oracles against foreign nations present us with a laundry list of specific causes that will bring about the Lord's punishment. As the Lord roars through Amos, delineating the transgressions of the foreign nations, the people of Israel are brought closer and closer to their own moment of realization. We are witness to a tight sequence of cause and effect where one pressure

20. Ibid., 188.

builds upon another, bringing about the crux of the drama in an unmistakable pattern.

LET JUSTICE ROLL DOWN (AMOS 5:21–24)

The oracle of Amos 5:21–24 contains perhaps the best-known words of the entire book. Near parallels to this oracle suggest that it represents a selection from a cultural stock recognizable as such to the prophetic audience.[21] Susan Niditch concludes that the Isaiah parallel (1:10–20) was part of a sermon that was performed.[22] Her work provides a very helpful backdrop to our examination of Amos. As a performed selection from a cultural stock of recognizable material, we are looking at a good example of a segment of dramatic activity.[23] As we noted earlier, via Beckerman, the process of selection and feedback that occurs between writers, performers, and spectators generates recurrent activities that are satisfying to all involved in the performative experience. What results is a representative collection of activities that are modified from age to age depending on the social context of the performance and its setting. These patterns of dramatic activity have a direct correspondence to performance activities: sermonizing, prophesying, debating, and so forth.

The Isa 1:10–20 passage resides within a larger literary unit that covers verses 4–20. Niditch concludes that this unit was a performed sermon. The sermon is persuasive and "displays a very high density of second person address, three rhetorical questions, numerous imperatives, three examples of the first person plural, and one cohortative."[24] These persuasive techniques are designed to give reason for the speaker to believe that "his audience will make the right decision, that is, the decision he wants them to make."[25]

The techniques that Isaiah uses to accomplish this rhetorical goal sound very much like the markers that designate the presence of a performance arena: (1) the use of imperatives, (2) the inclusion of the audience by means

---

21. See 1 Sam 15:22–23; Ps 50:7–23; Isa 1:10–20.

22. Susan Niditch, "The Composition of Isaiah 1," *Biblica* 6 (1980): 509–29.

23. Dramatic activity, segments, and the process by which activity becomes "set" into dramatic form are also explored in chapters 2 and 4, particularly through the process of selection and feedback.

24. Niditch, "Composition of Isaiah 1," 515.

25. Ibid., 514.

of a call to bear witness, a softer call to repentance, rhetorical questions that create a dialogue between listener and speaker, and (3) variation between third, second, and first person, with the effect of producing an ebb and flow to the pace of the performance, all fit nicely into already identified characteristics of a performance arena. These characteristics are found with greater density in Isa 1:4–20 than what can be found in the surrounding passages, leading to Niditch's contention that 1:4–20 is the literary remnant of a performed sermon. Niditch suggests here that the performed sermon displays a clear *project.* The speaker, by employing the strategies of second person address, rhetorical questions, and imperatives, is moving his spectators along the trajectory of his project so that they will make the decision he wants them to make.

Our interest in the Isa 1:10–20 passage rests in the fact that it has interesting parallels elsewhere in the Hebrew Bible (one of those being Amos 5:22–24), and the fact . . . that repetition may point to the existence of a formulaic pattern that provided the template for these parallel texts.[26] Niditch has analyzed the parallel texts and identifies the following pattern:[27]

1. A speech against the meaninglessness of the cult (1 Sam 15:22a–b; Amos 5:21–23; Ps 50:7–13; Isa 1:10–15)
2. The prophet's exhortation to mend one's ways through worship of God through proper adherence to the covenant (1 Sam 15:22c–d; Amos 5:24; Ps 50:14–15; Isa 1:16–17)
3. Offering the listener a choice between blessings and curses (Ps 50:16–23; Isa 1:18–20)

Based upon her analysis of Isa 1:4–20, Niditch claims that the style of the speaker of this text "which involves, exhorts, and engages his audience is that of a sermon while his choice and ordering of content as well as language used to present the content strongly suggest his participation in an oral tradition which enabled him to compose extemporaneously."[28]

---

26. A. B. Lord, *Singer of Tales* (New York: Atheneum, 1965), identifies the presence of formulaic material as one indicator of an oral prehistory to the text.

27. Niditch, "Composition of Isaiah 1," 517.

28. Ibid., 521.

If one of the parallel passages to Amos 5:22–24 can be considered a performed sermon, are we too far off the mark to wonder if Amos 5 is also susceptible to performance criticism? This is particularly so if we see the performed sermon in the whole context of dramatic activity. Dramatic activity is an activity of appearance. Says Beckerman, "It is always representing an event, a state of being, an idea that is not or, more likely, cannot be revealed directly."[29] In the case of Isaiah, as in the case of Amos, it is the scribe working to create the appearance of the prophet. The sermon is the performative device through which the scribe pursues the prophet's project. By exhorting, persuading, questioning, threatening, or any number of techniques he can employ to render the project of the prophet, the scribe-as-actor enters into the inner life of the prophetic drama in order to make this inner life appear to the spectators.

Dramatic activity can be natural or artificial, everyday behavior or behavior constructed specifically for dramatic purposes. Implicit in the claim that we can identify stock activities in prophetic texts is the notion that techniques and devices such as the sermon were artificial activities for the characters, or speakers, of these sermons and the spectators who witnessed scribal performances. In the case of natural dramatic activity, writes Beckerman, "we expect the appearance of everyday behavior, if not everyday circumstance. . . . Even when we witness unusual behavior, such as the ravings of inmates in a mental institution, we accept that behavior as a fair representation of happenings in a historical time and place."[30] Artificial activities are products of an artistic tradition and refer spectators not to personal experience but to socioaesthetic conventions.[31] In the case of sermons, and in the case of the oracles as well, we seem to have a combination of natural and artificial activity by virtue of the fact that what may have been natural to the prophet (e.g., preaching, delivering oracles, visions) is transformed into the product of a written tradition by the scribe.

29. Beckerman, *Dynamics of Drama*, 22.

30. Ibid.

31. Ibid., 23.

THE AMOS DOXOLOGIES

One of the long-standing problems that has plagued biblical scholars working on the book of Amos is the presence and placement of three doxologies (or hymnic fragments) scattered throughout the book. These doxologies appear at 4:13; 5:8–9; and 9:5–6. They interrupt the flow of the text and seem to be out of place. That there is some connection between them is supported by the fact that all three share a common participial construction and the phrase "The LORD is his name."

The closest parallel to these doxologies in other biblical literature is found in Job 9:5–10, but even this comparison is not close enough to conclude that the Amos material and the Job material stem from the same stock of traditional literature. Most commentators believe that the Amos doxologies are relatively late in origin,[32] and the purpose for their insertion into the book of Amos is disputed. One commentator believes that the hymn in 9:5–6 marked a "shorter ending" of the book of Amos,[33] and another commentator believes the first two doxologies (4:13 and 5:8–9) mark off the "middle of the younger book of Amos."[34] Both agree that the placement of the three fragments is intentional[35] and that the real question is not about how the three doxologies functioned prior to their placement in Amos, but how they function now, having been properly placed by the scribe or redactor.

Hans Walter Wolff has brought attention to the fact that the first two doxologies are situated in close proximity to the mention of "Bethel."[36] The

32. James Crenshaw, *Hymnic Affirmation of Divine Justice: The Doxologies of Amos and Related Texts in the Old Testament* (Missoula, Mont.: Published by Scholars Press for the Society of Biblical Literature, 1975), 25ff. See also F. Horst, "Die Doxologien im Amosbuch," *Zeitschrift für die alttestamentliche Wissenschaft* 47 (1929): 45–54.

33. See K. Koch, "Die Rolle der hymnischen Abschnitte in der Komposition des Amos-Buches," *Zeitschrift für die alttestamentliche Wissenschaft* 86 (1974): 504–37.

34. Jorg Jeremias, *The Book of Amos* (Old Testament Library; Louisville, Ky.: Westminster John Knox, 1998), 78.

35. Most but not all scholars agree that the doxologies are placed intentionally. One commentator suggests that the doxologies simply make up for lost Amos material. K. Budde, "Zur Geschichte des Buches Amos," *Studien zur semitischen Philologie und Religionsgeschichte: Julius Wellhausen zum siebzigsten Geburtstag* (Beihefte zur Zeitschrift für die alttestamentliche Wissenschaft 27; Giessen: Topelmann, 1914), 106.

36. Hans Walter Wolff, *Joel and Amos* (trans. Waldemar Janzen, S. Dean McBride, and Charles Muenchow; Hermeneia; Philadelphia: Fortress, 1977), 218ff. See also E. Sellin and G. Fohrer, *Introduction to the Old Testament* (trans. D. Green; Nashville: Abingdon, 1968), 193.

sustaining power of God displayed in the universe at large is also the power brought to bear in judgment upon a cult determined to be idolatrous and unjust. The doxologies make clear to the reader/audience just who it is that wields power to both sustain and to judge: Yahweh is his name.[37] Shalom Paul believes this extolling of God and his manifest power in all creation to be the central function of the hymns. He sees no reason to doubt their originality, nor does he see reason to limit the hymns to a focused polemic against Bethel.[38] The hymns, or fragments of one hymn, provide powerful imagery by which to emphasize the role of Yahweh in world events.

A performance analysis of the placement of the doxologies within the book of Amos makes this function even clearer. The idea of an Amos performance has already been hinted at by an earlier commentator. K. Cramer is of the opinion that the hymnic fragments are authentic to the Amos pronouncements and in fact may represent the most important parts of the prophet's message, which were sung to the listening audience.[39] If Cramer is right, at a strategic location within the book we have a score from a musical performance that can now be analyzed as a performance.

Karl Moller envisions a performance of a different sort. He suggests that the hymnic fragments progressively intensify the image of God's destructive abilities, concluding with a global cry of mourning.[40] This progression, claims Moller, fits quite nicely with

> our conception of the book as a presentation of the debate between Amos and his audience. In his struggle to convince people that divine judgment will befall them, Amos is presented as having employed increasingly drastic images of Yahweh, his power and actions and the implications this will have for those who are the targets of his punishment.[41]

---

37. Jeremias, *Book of Amos*, 80.

38. Paul, *Amos*, 155–56.

39. K. Cramer, *Amos—Versuch einer theologischen Interpretation* (Beiträge zur Wissenschaft vom Alten und Neuen Testament 15; Stuttgart: Kohlhammer, 1930), 93.

40. Karl Moller, "'Hear This Word Against You': A Fresh Look at the Arrangement and the Rhetorical Strategy of the Book of Amos," *Vetus Testamentum* 50 (2000): 514.

41. Ibid., 514–15.

While the actual debate between the prophet and his audience may be beyond reconstruction, we believe that Moller is quite right in conceptualizing the hymnic fragments as a performance. Even further, Moller's suggestion that the hymnic fragments are part of an increasingly drastic set of images of the Lord used as a strategy for enhancing the prophet's project to convince his spectators that divine judgment will befall them supports the argument that we are dealing with an intensive mode of drama.

Intensive modes of drama are the products of specific causes. The segments of intensive modes of drama reveal a clear pattern of causation, which determines how one segment will depend on another.[42] The logic of a pattern of causation not only applies to the literary form of intensive modes of drama, but to the performative structure as well. A character's project, his intentions and motivations, are also guided by principles of logic. Moller's suggestion that the doxologies are part of a pattern of strategies used by the prophet to convince his spectators that divine judgment will befall them if they do not listen makes perfect sense from the performance point of view, perhaps even more so if they were sung or chanted. The limits of the speaking voice can be transcended by opening up the voice in song. On a purely practical level, resonance, volume, and the expressive dynamics of the voice are enhanced by singing or chanting. Additionally, the variety and intensity this can add to performance increases the performer's ability to sustain the interest of the spectators. Interestingly, in the doxologies we have the prophet speaking solely in his own voice, rather than speaking as God, which he does in the oracles and in the sermon. This would further intensify the causal relationship between who God is and his ability to determine the fate of the spectators. Speaking *about* God rather than *as* God, Amos reminds his spectators of what knowledge they all share: "The LORD, the God of hosts, is his name!" In this crucial moment, their shared past with the Lord God of hosts links them inextricably together.

> If a particular moment of human experience can be considered the nexus of a life cycle, the most meaningful actions of life are therefore the most critical. But if critical actions

42. Beckerman, *Dynamics of Drama*, 175.

> are effects of the past, man is a prisoner of his past. He is caught in a highly contracted situation, his end foretold before the plot begins, for the plot is enmeshed in the toils of story.[43]

In the story of the Lord's relationship to the people of Israel, the drama of Amos is but one intensely focused look at that relationship. Within the structure of this drama we have identified a variety of performance structures (oracles, sermon, visions, doxologies) that are part of the conventional structure of the scribe's text, or script. Each of these structures participates, in its own way, in the generation of the prophet's overall project: to make believers out of the people of Israel. The plot of the Amos drama is part of the larger past: God's relationship to his people.

For the scribe, the prophet Amos was a living link between the past, the present, and the future. When he prophesied, he was the human link between the Lord, the witnesses of his prophecy, and the eternal present of that relationship. What is most fascinating about the scribe-as-performer, rendering the character of the prophet through his performance, is his ability to represent that same crucial moment in the relationship between the Lord and his people, linking the past, present, and future of his own spectators through the characters of Amos and his spectators. This is the essence of dramatic activity.

Before turning to an examination of the vision reports in the next chapter, a brief summary of the performance structures we have explored to this point reveals a substantial range of techniques available to the scribe-as-actor to bring the Amos drama to life. Each contributes to the basic drama paradigm we explored in earlier chapters by providing the scribe-as-actor with multiple means for representing the character of the prophet, God, and the spectators present to the prophet.

43. Ibid., 187.

Dramatic Activity →	**Imagined Act** →	**Inner Life**
(What the actor does)	(What the character does)	(What is revealed)

The following table summarizes how these performance structures (oracles, sermons, doxologies) exemplify the basic drama paradigm through a variety of techniques.

Oracles	Sermon	Doxologies
Sustained segments marked by movement between prophet-as-character and God-as-character, requiring the scribe to effectively transition between the characters. As these occur right at the beginning of the book of Amos, the scribe-as-actor introduces the characters (sets the stage for the drama) and launches into the drama late in the story of the people of Israel. An intensive mode of drama is established when the Lord roars like a lion.	A speech in which a scribe, through the character of the prophet, assumes the character of God and speaks directly to the spectators at hand. The level of confrontation and direct connection is high. "I hate," "I take no delight," "I will not accept," "I will not look upon," "I will not listen"—God's refusal to accept, to look upon, or to listen delivered by a live human being (scribe-as-actor) is a refusal to enter into a relationship on human terms, that is, to see, to hear, and to accept the other.	Though lacking the direct, intensive, confrontational mode of both the oracles and the sermon, the doxologies present the character of the prophet in human terms; he is one of the spectators even though he is a foreigner. He speaks, as a mortal, of what all mortals know about God: that he is the God of life and of destruction. If sung or chanted, they also introduce another layer of performance skill that would help to create the variety and intensity required to sustain the spectators' attention.

CHAPTER SIX

Amos 7–9: The Vision Reports

The series of visions in Amos 7–9 provides an interesting opportunity to apply several of the concepts drawn from performance criticism. In particular, the dramatic notions of project, precipitating context, and action can be employed usefully in the analysis of these vision reports.

It is not unusual for commentators on the prophetic literature of the Hebrew Bible to recognize the dramatic associations found in their material. A recent introduction to Zephaniah by Paul House includes that very acknowledgment in the title of the work.[1] Brian Peckham says of the prophets Isaiah, Amos, and Hosea, "Together their compositions reveal the range, repertory, and traditional characterizations of an educated, inspired, and theatrical milieu."[2] While some have recognized the "theatrical milieu," few have seriously analyzed it.[3] Perhaps the most extensive investigation is that by

1. Paul House, *Zephaniah: A Prophetic Drama,* JSOTSup 69 (Sheffield, England: Sheffield Academic Press, 1989).

2. Brian Peckham, *History and Prophecy: The Development of Late Judean Literary Traditions* (Anchor Bible Reference Library; New York: Doubleday, 1993), 134.

3. Georg Fohrer and Ernst Sellin have provided a summary description of symbolic prophetic action and speech in *Introduction to the Old Testament* (Nashville: Abingdon Press, 1958), 356. Also, Bernard Lang compares some prophetic activities to "street theater." See Lang, *Monotheism and the*

(continued)

David Stacey. Although it is very helpful in suggesting analytical tools, it is restricted to a treatment of forty-eight passages narrating prophetic actions.[4] In some significant ways, this chapter is a continuation of Stacey's work, applying some of his analysis to passages that he could not investigate and positing certain refinements of the analytical tools that he suggests.[5]

Whenever an analysis like this is undertaken, the danger is always present that the analytical tool will be viewed as an end in itself and the elucidation of the text will be subsumed under the presentation of the tool. This danger is particularly present here, since dramatic analysis necessarily deals with the relationship between an act or speech and the meaning of that act or speech, and we can never be certain that we have got it right when applying that analysis to a culture so separated from us as that of the prophets.[6] Nevertheless, if the enquiry yields a fresh insight or a new set of questions that give a clearer understanding of the world of the prophet, then the journey will have been worthwhile.[7]

Stacey offers a definition of material in the Hebrew Bible that is suscep-

---

3. (continued) *Prophetic Minority* (Sheffield: Almond, 1983), 81ff.; and Lang, "Street Theater: Raising the Dead and the Zoroastrian Connection in Ezekiel's Prophecy," in *Ezekiel and His Book* (ed. J. Lust; Bibliotheca ephemeridum theologicarum lovaniensium 74; Leuven: Peeters, 1986), 297–316. The utilization of new tools and new questions in the examination of the Hebrew prophets is evidenced by a number of recent articles and monographs, including Ferdinand Deist, "The Prophets: Are We Heading for a Paradigm Shift?" in *This Place Is too Small for Us: The Israelite Prophets in Recent Scholarship*, ed. Robert Gordon (Winona Lake, Ind.: Eisenbrauns, 1995); Hans Barstad, "No Prophets?: Recent Developments in Biblical Prophecy Research and Ancient Near Eastern Prophecy," JSOT 57 (1993), 39–60; J. M. Ward, "The Eclipse of the Prophet in Contemporary Prophetic Studios," *Union Seminary Quarterly Review* 42 (1988): 97–104; and Ehud Ben Zvi and Michael Floyd, "Introduction: Writings, Speeches, and the Prophetic Books—Setting an Agenda" in *Writings and Speech in Israelite and Ancient Near Eastern Prophecy*, ed. Ehud Ben Zvi and Michael Floyd (Atlanta: Society of Biblical Literature, 2000), 1–30. In addition, a dissertation by Joyce Louise Wood applies dramatic theory to a discussion of the redaction of the Amos prophecy. See Wood, "Amos: Prophecy as a Performing Art and Its Transformation in Book Culture" (Ph.D. diss.; St. Michael's College and Biblical Department of the Toronto School of Theology, 1993).

4. See David Stacey, *Prophetic Drama in the Old Testament* (London: Epworth, 1990); and Stacey, "The Function of Prophetic Drama," in *This Place Is Too Small for Us: The Israelite Prophets in Recent Scholarship* (ed. R. Gordon; Winona Lake, Ind.: Eisenbrauns, 1995).

5. Stacey recognizes the need to investigate passages beyond the scope of his study and mentions specifically those that we treat here. Stacey, *Prophetic Drama in the Old Testament*, 64.

6. See Thomas W. Overholt, "Prophecy: The Problem of Cross-Cultural Comparison," *Semeia* 21 (1982): 55–78.

7. See Thomas W. Overholt, *Prophecy in Cross-Cultural Perspective* (Atlanta: Scholars Press, 1986).

tible to investigation as drama by describing "prophetic action that goes beyond the functional and that is reckoned to signify something beyond itself."[8] Vision reports form prime material for dramatic investigation. Unlike the prophetic act, which is effective independently of its recounting, the vision is effective only if it is reported. Stacey goes even further: "When an oracle passes from the spoken to the written, it gains in force and validity."[9] We then are concerned with the function of the written form of the vision report.[10] How did it function to aid the message delivered by the prophet? Moreover, how did the vision report, now incorporated into a formal document, effectively function as part of the audience response to the prophetic event?

DRAMA PARADIGMS

Under the wide umbrella of Aristotle's *Poetics* a number of historically located definitions of drama have evolved.[11] The two classical positions of Greek dramatists Aeschylus and Euripides continue to represent the extremes of the drama continuum. Aeschylus represents the traditional Greek position that the poet is a moral teacher and his work must fulfill a moral purpose. Euripides represents a position, currently in vogue, that art's function is the revelation of reality, aside from moral and ethical questions.[12] Across this continuum, from moral didacticism to revelation and representation, there are universally acknowledged components of the drama that are essential to dramatic form and ultimately dramatic action, comprising the true force of the drama.

Drama occurs when one or more human beings isolated in time and space

---

8. Stacey, *Prophetic Drama in the Old Testament*, 64.

9. Ibid., 232.

10. Wood is of the opinion that a dramatic form is present throughout the structure of the Amos literature. Wood, "Amos," 505.

11. An excellent historical survey of major theories of drama is Marvin Carlson, *Performance: A Critical Introduction* (New York: Routledge, 2003). Other valuable sources offering fundamental theories of drama include the works of Bernard Dukore, *Dramatic Theory and Criticism: Greeks to Grotowski* (New York: Holt, Rinehart & Winston, 1974); Francis Fergusson, *The Idea of Theatre* (New York: Doubleday Anchor, 1994); and Martin Esslin, *An Anatomy of Drama* (New York: Hill and Wang, 1976).

12. Marvin Carlson, *Theories of the Theatre: A Historical and Critical Survey from the Greeks to the Present* (Ithaca, N.Y.: Cornell University Press, 1984), 15.

present themselves in imagined acts to another or others. Primary to the function and impact of drama is the acknowledgment that, as a form of theatre, drama is completely dependent on the presence of human beings. Eliminate the human presence and you eliminate theatre. As something that occurs, drama is in the eternal present. Dramatic time is the time of now, even when it conventionally represents the past, the future, or a time only imagined. This was also true for Aristotle, whose famous definition of *tragedy* reminds us that tragedy takes "the form of action," meaning that it is acted on a stage, or that it occurs, isolated in time and space, as an exchange between performer and audience.[13]

In the relationship between performer, audience, and act, a schematic framework emerges.[14] A central element of this framework is the imagined act, or what the actor does that brings to life the virtual existence of the world of the drama. Though we used this visual representation earlier, it will be helpful to repeat it here:

Activity (what the actor does)

↓

Imagined Act (what the character does)

↓

Inner Life (what the imagined act reveals)

13. All references to the *Poetics* are taken from *Aristotle's Poetics* (trans. S. H. Butcher; New York: Hill & Wang, 1994). Francis Fergusson discusses Aristotle's definition of tragedy in his introductory essay, "The Idea of Theatre."

14. In chapter 3 we developed the relationship between dramatic activity, the imagined act, and the inner life of the drama. This relationship is the result of a performable scheme emerging from the written script through the modes of presentation developed by the performer.

In the case of the prophetic dramas, what is enacted is not actuality but a schematic notion of actuality that the audience will recognize. These imagined acts form the body of dramatic activity or the flesh on the bones of what we would usually refer to as the plot. Imagined acts are not what they seem, but are a surrogate for some other activity, whether historical, mythical, or fanciful.[15] Dramatic activity, argues Beckerman, "is always representing an event, a state of being, an idea that is not or, more likely, cannot be revealed directly."[16] The scribe, as both writer and actor of the drama, does not have the ability to reveal the event directly as the prophet did. He must rely on his ability to create the drama and have it point to the event itself.

The range of dramatic activity from which the dramatist makes choices is as broad as the range of conventionalized human activities. From Oedipus plucking out his eyes with a brooch, to King Lear looking for signs of Cordelia's breath on the surface of a mirror, to Willie Loman's visions of his dead brother in Arthur Miller's *Death of a Salesman,* dramatic activity is a schematic notion that can be readily perceived by the audience. The function of dramatic activity is to liberate the spirit by juxtaposing "a human being in his total physical being with an imagined act to produce an illusion of actuality."[17] For the scribe who enacted the drama of Amos, the oracles, visions, sermon, and doxologies form the primary schematic of presentation. The imagined act, an expression of the imagination of the dramatist, must be viewed in Gadamer's terms as "a creative force which enables one to find questions worth asking in the new context."[18]

Dramatic activity reveals an act-scheme (presentational forms) existing on the level of the theatrical conventions of a given period and the immediate act of presentation witnessed by the audience. What the act-scheme represents or

15. Beckerman argues that a play uses modes of activity conventionalized by the historical era in which it is written (*Dynamics of Drama,* 22–23). Beckerman is certainly not alone in this position (see especially Esslin, *An Anatomy of Drama,* 95–105). His notion of conventionalized modes of activity extends beyond the theater to social, political, and economic conventions as well.

16. Beckerman, *Dynamics of Drama,* 22.

17. Ibid.

18. H. G. Gadamer, "Die Universalität des hermeneutischen Problems," in *Kleine Scarifien I: Philosohpie Hermeneutik* (Tübigen, Germany: Mohr, 1967), quoted in Stacey, *Prophetic Drama in the Old Testament,* 8.

signifies is the act-image.[19] The act-image is an elusive concept. Like Aristotle's concept of action, the act-image is more than the deeds, events, or physical activity of the act-scheme. It is what is revealed to the spectator when all the elements of the drama come together in the act of presentation. Francis Fergusson describes action (praxis) as "the motivation from which deeds spring."[20] He quotes S. H. Butcher: "The praxis that art seeks to reproduce is mainly a psychic energy working outwards."[21]

Beckerman's act-image offers an explanation of how that "working outwards" happens. He suggests that "what we accept as representation actually consists of signs that are related in a fundamentally schematic manner."[22] These signs are effective contextually. Take the example of a character dying on stage. There is certainly not one set of activities that will signify death to an audience. However, there are a limited number of motions, sounds, and sequences that stand for "natural signs of dying but that are not true significations in themselves."[23] These contextual, conventionalized schemes are both the portrayal of actual skill on the part of the performer and of a virtual existence to which the performer points. "In a broad sense," writes Beckerman, "the act-scheme [and the resulting act-image] has a dynamic, though not necessarily causative, connection to the encompassing code."[24]

---

19. Bernard Beckerman, *Theatrical Presentation: Performer, Audience, and Act* (ed. Gloria Brim Beckerman and William Coco; New York: Routledge, 1990), 101. Beckerman's notion of the act-image clarifies the relationship Aristotle establishes between the organic and inorganic "parts" of the tragedy. Here again, rather than simply describing the parts of the drama, Beckerman offers an explanation for how the drama functions. Martin Esslin offers an explanation of dramatic activity that has some resonance with Beckerman as well. However, in *An Anatomy of Drama*, Esslin focuses more on the literary implications of dramatic structure while Beckerman focuses on the performative. Francis Fergusson, in *The Idea of Theatre*, also resonates with Beckerman, arguing that the forms of our lives, like the forms of our art, depend on what we believe to be real (32). However, Fergusson's book is a philosophical exploration of the essence of theater and not an examination of the theater as performed event. As Beckerman writes, "In talking about a play, we usually discuss its act-image (plot and story) rather than its act-scheme (presentational forms)." Beckerman, *Theatrical Presentation*, 101.

20. Francis Fergusson, *The Idea of Theatre* (New York: Doubleday Anchor, 1994), 8.

21. S. H. Butcher, *Aristotle's Theory of Poetry and Fine Arts* (4th ed.; New York: Hill and Wang, 1961), quoted in Ibid.

22. Beckerman, *Theatrical Presentation*, 102.

23. Ibid.

24. Ibid., 105. See page 99, note 40 on individual and collective audiences. By their very nature, dramas abstract from human experience, refining that abstraction into a "pure analogue of a larger reality."

The code, or governing conditions of performance in a given period, largely determines the kind of act-schemes a culture will produce. The conditions of performance influence a number of things from scale, length of performance, variety of performance, and subject matter. The governing conditions of performance (the code), act-schemes (acts in the form that they play before us), and act-images (what the act-scheme signifies or represents), form the analytical framework for dealing with a conception of the dramas as events that occur, events such as the prophetic dramas of the Hebrew Bible.

THE AMOS VISION REPORTS

There are two versions of prophetic drama. One version occurs when the prophet acts out and the record of that action is reported as such in the prophetic literature.[25] The other version consists of prophetic vision reports. In the vision, a drama is being played out. It simply is visible only to the prophet and must await his retelling for it to be available to a wider audience.[26] In both versions of prophetic drama, there are several shared characteristics.

First, the potency of the prophetic dramas is contingent upon the "dynamic nature of the person who carries them out."[27] That is, prophetic drama draws its potency from the social power of the prophet.[28] And that social power seems to be, at least in part, contingent upon the prophet's ability to represent the word of the Lord. That ability to re-present leads to

---

25. Stacey, *Prophetic Drama in the Old Testament*, has a list of forty-eight dramatic events. Compare this to A. Van den Born, *Profetie Metterdaad* (Roermond: Maaseik, 1947), 14–15, which lists thirty-two; and A. W. Groenman, *Het Karakter van de Symbolische Handelingen der Oud-Testamentische Profeten* (Haarlem: H. D. Tjeenk Willink, 1942), 8ff., which lists 31. George Fohrer, *History of Israelite Religion* (trans. David Green; Nashville: Abingdon, 1972), 240, lists twenty-eight "symbolic actions" found in thirty-two texts. Of the events on these lists, only about twenty are common to all.

26. When presented in a text, the prophetic vision is subject to a secondary layer of presentation. In the text, the prophet becomes a character in the vision of the scribe. The project of the scribe subsumes that of the prophet. James Linville, writing about the vision reports of Amos, concludes, "In my view, the character of the prophet is used as a tool within these few chapters to aid in the reader's self-identification in the text, to feel the terror of the divine word. Amos is a tool of the writers, and is a role assumed by the reader." Linville, "Visions and Voices: Amos 7–9," *Biblica* 80 (1999): 41.

27. Stacey, *Prophetic Drama in the Old Testament*, 60.

28. In chapter 2 we discussed the process by which the scribe appropriates the social power of the prophet.

the second characteristic of prophetic drama. The dramas were performed, whether in act or vision, at the direction of the Lord.[29] The prophets believed that they were being directed by a higher power, and their effectiveness depended upon their ability to make their audience arrive at the same conclusion. The dramas, says Stacey, "point away from themselves towards an unseen element."[30] The third characteristic of prophetic drama is that it was not ritualized. Prophetic dramas seem to have been for one particular audience at one particular time. To be sure, they make use of traditional elements, but in such a way as to make application of the tradition to a particular time and place.[31]

Part of the prophetic drama that occurs in the book of Amos is in the form of vision reports. The vision reports (7:1–3, 4–6, 7–9; 8:1–3; 9:1–4) are concise and may have figured prominently into the structuring of the book: oracles in the first part of the book followed by visions in the second half.[32] Although the reports follow a well-defined form, with an introductory formula followed by a report of the vision and concluding with an explanatory oration made by either the prophet or the Lord, there is room for variation in both form and contextual placement.[33] The vision report can be followed by the succeeding vision, a narrative, or a judgment oracle.

The vision reports fit very well the description of drama we have established throughout this book.[34] Four of the five reports consist of time-bound and space-specific actions that are unified and explained by a short story line. Aeschylus's conception of dramatic structure also can be applied to the vision

29. Stacey, *Prophetic Drama in the Old Testament*, 61.

30. Ibid., 260.

31. Ibid., 62.

32. This structure is hinted at in the opening verse of Amos. The vision report itself may have an important social function in preserving the memory of the charismatic authority of the prophet. See Ronald Clements, "Max Weber, Charisma, and Biblical Prophecy," in *Prophecy and Prophets: The Diversity of Contemporary Issues in Scholarship* (ed. Y. Gitay; Semeia Studies; Atlanta: Scholars Press, 1997), 89–108.

33. The redactional history of the vision reports, as evidenced by the variations in form, need not concern us here, for our immediate goal is to analyze the final form of the report within the context of the prophetic book. For a discussion of the prophetic literature and its relationship to the prophet himself, see A. Auld, "Prophets through the Looking Glass: Between Writings and Moses," *Journal for the Study of the Old Testament* 27 (1983): 3–23.

34. Burke Long identified this association in "Reports of Visions among the Prophets," in *Journal of Biblical Literature* 95 (1976): 359–60.

reports of Amos, for when viewed as five acts within one drama, the reports contain a plot, a conflict, and a resultant climax.[35]

Vision 1 (7:1–3): The Locusts. The plot of this drama is brief and powerful. The prophet observes the Lord while in the process of forming a devastating plague of locusts bent on devouring the grass of the land and so depriving the inhabitants of Jacob the means to survive. Two characters appear in conflict: the Lord and Amos, the prophet. Having observed the preparations of the Lord, the prophet assumes the role of advocate and pleads for pardon on behalf of the endangered and unsuspecting population. The prophet is persuasive and the Lord relents.

Vision 2 (7:4–6): The Unquenchable Fire. The plot of the second vision is like that of the first. Once again, two characters stand in conflict: the Lord and Amos. This time, the Lord is preparing an unquenchable fire to devour the land and all those who live on it. Once again, the prophet pleads for the survival of the people by begging the Lord to stop preparing for judgment. And once again, the conflict is resolved when the Lord acquiesces to the prophet and abandons his preparations.

Vision 3 (7:7–9): The Wall. The plot of this dramatic vision is different from those just preceding, and it shares significant characteristics with the dramatic vision to follow (8:1–3). Once again, however, there are two actors, the Lord and Amos. This time the conflict becomes oblique. The Lord simply asks the prophet to describe what he observes, and based upon that observation the Lord pronounces a judgment over the people Israel and in particular their religious and political institutions. The prophet stands mute in the presence of this revelation, and it is he who must acquiesce.

Vision 4 (8:1–3): Summer Fruit. This dramatic vision follows the same plot as that of the previous vision. Once again, the two actors, the Lord and the prophet, engage in no direct conflict. The conflict has become covert, existing in the form of audience anxiety: "The time is ripe for my people Israel; I will spare them no longer" (NIV). The prophet is asked to describe what he

---

35. Paul House, *Zephaniah, A Prophetic Drama* (Journal for the Study of the Old Testament: Supplement Series 69; Sheffield: Sheffield Academic Press, 1989), 44. House identifies a subgenre of drama that has useful application to biblical studies. He defines "closet drama" as drama that "exists as art without being presented" (50). It is literature that has dramatic characteristics (e.g., plot, character) but need not have been staged. However, as we have demonstrated through performance criticism, the drama of Amos contains more than the literary features of a dramatic text.

sees, and the observation is used as a platform from which to describe an impending judgment. Similar to the dramatic episode of 7:7–9, the dialogue lends an air of finality to the judgment pronounced, for both dramatic visions proclaim that this is the last visitation that the Lord will make upon the people Israel.

Vision 5 (9:1–4) Divine Soliloquy. This final dramatic vision is unlike all that have come before. Only one actor, the Lord, is present. There is no plot, no conflict, and no resolution. There is only a dreadful divine soliloquy of complete and final judgment. The act-image is now clearly revealed, stripped from all of its dramatic accoutrements. Those judgments, threatened by the act-schemes of the earlier scenes, have now become unalterably fixed so that there is no escape.

In this segment of the Amos drama, the visions function as the site where the action occurs. Implicitly or explicitly, Amos need only invoke the "Thus says the LORD," and the location of his visions, his dramatic imagination, is established. In fact, the prophet can be viewed as the actor/playwright. The prophet is granted social authority through the widespread recognition of his ability to personify the dramatic code; it is the prophet who prophesies. In preserving the visions as text, the social authority, as well as the historical significance of the prophet/character, is made available to later audiences in the recognizable form of the prophetic drama, a form of social authority now controlled by the scribe.[36]

These five visions reveal an act-scheme consisting of a dramatic structure very similar to that found in the extant Greek tragedies of fifth-century Athens. From the dialogue between the Lord God and Amos, a classic dyadic exchange, to the divine soliloquy of vision five, functioning as the final episode invoking Euripides' later use of the *Deus ex machina,* a schematic emerges in recognizable dramatic shape and function. Essentially, the visions reveal a distinctive intensive structure, as do the oracles against foreign nations. The visions offer the spectator a dimension of dramatic activity not found in the oracles. This added dimension is the dialogue between the Lord God and his prophet. In the oracles, Amos addresses the spectators directly either as prophet, or as God. In the vision reports, we *see and hear* Amos's

36. See the graphic description in chapter 2 of the relationship between the prophet, the scribe, and the character of the prophet presented to us in the Amos text.

dialogue with God. From a performance perspective, this would require the scribe, as reader/presenter of the text, to display a certain amount of performance skill. Even the simple transitions in the dialogue would require the scribe-as-actor to move between the characters of Amos and the Lord in such a way that the increasing intensity of the visions could be experienced by the spectators: "'What do you see Amos?' he asked. 'A basket of ripe fruit,' I answered. Then the LORD said to me, 'The time is ripe for my people Israel; I will spare them no longer'" (NIV). What we witness here is a very compact and simple exchange that varies from the preceding vision sequences where the prophet reports on what the Lord showed him and then begs the Lord to relent. Now the prophet and the Lord speak to each other in the form of a dialectical exchange:

The Lord queries Amos ⟶ Amos responds ⟶ The Lord pronounces judgment

This slight variation would be a critical moment to anyone dealing with the problem of how to present/perform this text. The fact that it occurs just after the Amos and Amaziah confrontation is very interesting, and we will offer an explanation rooted in performance criticism later in the chapter.

Each vision contains a single episode, or event, encompassing the complex relationship between the Lord, Amos, and the people of Israel, all articulated in an isolated situation. The hallmark of these visions is their simplicity and unity. Each vision is a self-contained whole developed around a single episode yet reaching ahead to the logic of the next. As dramatic events with structured act-schemes, they are concerned only with the bare essentials of the action.[37] With all narrative or prosaic distractions removed, the audience is forced to focus attention upon the essentials required to carry the plot of the drama. They are designed to move swiftly to the crux of the drama.

Audience awareness of the plot has been established by the oracles that

---

37. This was a key feature of dramatic structure until the Renaissance.

precede the visions. In no uncertain terms, the prophet has indicated that the Lord is preparing judgment for Israel. The series of dramatic visions remains focused on this one stream of events. This singular movement, from event to event, drives the action of the drama in the time of the present, moving quickly toward a crux that both resolves the conflict within the series of visions and allows recognition of a more complex plot previously addressed by the prophetic oracles. As with Amos's visions, the plot of the drama begins late in the action of the larger story. The "roaring of the lion" was heard early in the book, and that roar is now echoed in the finality of the judgment pronounced in vision 5.

Taken as a unit, the five visions form a structured whole operating on several formal levels. The basic dramatic activity of the first four visions sets up a rhythmic pattern essential to an act-scheme of forgiveness and judgment. Twice Amos is able to persuade the Lord not to destroy God's own people. Twice the Lord pronounces judgment predicated by Amos's observations. All is finally brought to a climax when only God stands on the stage of Amos's vision and pronounces a final judgment. This climactic pattern has the symmetrical balance, dialogic exchange, and the formality of a concluding event still present in much of the drama of our own century. Reading the visions as a drama places emphasis on the human experience of Amos and the people of Israel. Their vulnerability to the Lord is staged in Amos's visions, along with their dramatic role as the people of Israel. The act-scheme of forgiveness and judgment is predicated on an emerging character (the people of Israel) in relation to a source of action (the Lord). Visions 1 and 2 establish the possibility of tragedy, of death and destruction brought about by a force transcendent of the human being. Read as drama, these visions are rooted in one of the most primal and basic human experiences: terror.

Visions 3 and 4 establish a vector, or developing path of tension, that points the audience to consider the Lord's judgment over the religious and political institutions of the people of Israel. These middle visions, placed after the establishment of plot and before the climactic resolution, occupy a distinctive place in the structure of the drama. Placed as the last scenes before the drama ends, these two visions carry the extra weight of functioning as the drama's crux. In the complex plots Aristotle favored, the third and fourth episodes often contained the reversal of the hero's fortunes and the moment of recognition, or failure of recognition, which set up the end of the drama.

Such is the case in this series of dramatic visions. The prophet's acquiescence to the determined judgments of the Lord indicates that moment of recognition in which the character must accept the unalterable resolution made clear in the final act. At this moment in the drama the consequences of being human and of being the people of Israel are made most clear. The prophet is now compelled to act, to describe what he observes to the Lord. His words, describing the actions of the people of Israel, become the thing upon which the Lord acts in return. Amos resembles the Greek tragic heroes who, following the moment of recognition, must publicly profess what they have seen and done as an integral part of the climax and resolution of the drama. In doing so, Amos brings the tragic rhythm of the drama to the final moment of judgment.

Vision 5, the Lord's divine soliloquy, completes the movement of the action begun in vision 1 and developed in discrete episodes through visions 2, 3, and 4. The logic of the vision episodes is only fulfilled by the singular presence of the Lord on the stage of Amos's prophetic drama, a stage representing (act-image) the religious, political, and social institutions (act-scheme) of the people of Israel. The Lord's final judgment completes the logic of the drama's action. God stands alone on the stage of Israel's very existence with a view from which none can hide. The terror of the earlier visions now turns to trembling as the Lord strikes the final chord of feeling in the drama. The scheme of the action is realized; the culprit (the people of Israel) is found in order to purify human life.

THE AMOS-AMAZIAH CONFRONTATION (7:10–17)

The narrative of 7:10–17 has long posed a problem for commentators on the book of Amos. The plain fact is that it appears to be out of place.[38] The narrative is placed square in the middle of a series of visions that are very clearly linked together both stylistically and thematically. So the question is, Why here? Why does the Amos narrative appear where it does, and what is the function of the narrative given its present location within the book?

There have been several notable attempts to explain the location of the

38. See J. Alberto Soggin, *The Prophet Amos: A Translation and Commentary* (London: SCM Press, 1987), 125.

Amos narrative. L. Eslinger argues that the placement of the narrative is a pivotal turning point for the prophet. In the visions prior to the conflict with Amaziah, Amos pleads that the coming judgment be suspended or withheld altogether. After the narrative, however, there is no such objection from the prophet, as he seems to acquiesce to the inevitability of God's punishment upon Israel.[39]

Karl Moller believes that the location of the Amos narrative is strategically placed and adds to the development of the book. In its present location, the narrative "links Amaziah's intervention to the Amos conspiratory statement of 7:9."[40] That is, the prophet's announcement of judgment by the sword upon the royal house of Jeroboam, in 7:9, leads to the priest's conclusion of conspiracy vocalized in 7:10 and his consequent banishment of the prophet from the royal sanctuary at Bethel and from the land of Israel itself. But, according to Moller, the controversy between Amaziah and Amos plays another role. Moller believes that the book of Amos is structured as a public debate between the prophet and his spectators. In 7:10–17, Amaziah functions, as it were, as the personification of the audience, and his reaction to Amos represents the reaction of the original audience. Moller concludes that "throughout the book the audience's reactions to the prophet's ministry are mostly (though not always) implied, in vii 10–17 the reaction by one of its (more influential) members is reported in some detail."[41]

Applying performance criticism to the narrative can lead us a bit farther down the path suggested by Moller. The narrative is every bit a vision report, as are the surrounding five visions. For the narrative, however, it is the scribe that is reporting the vision and the prophet is now not an actor in the performance but a character in the scribal vision. As we have suggested throughout this book, the drama, as something that occurs, is structured according to segments of activity. These segments work together to allow the presentation of the drama to unfold before its spectators. Dramatic segments are structured around what can be called a major activity (e.g., delivering oracles, reporting visions), and, according to Beckerman, "An entire presentation is a segment of time differentiated from the preceding and succeeding surround-

39. L. Eslinger, "The Education of Amos," *Hebrew Annual Review* 11 (1987): 55.

40. Karl Moller, "'Hear This Word against You': A Fresh Look at the Arrangement and the Rhetorical Strategy of the Book of Amos," *Vetus Testamentum* 50 (2000): 516.

41. Ibid., 517.

ing time by the assemblage of an audience."[42] Each segment can be further subdivided into tasks, or individual activities, until we have a clear picture of precisely what is happening in the drama before us. Each of the tasks or activities that constitute the major activity of a segment is nested within the overall segment. Amos addresses his spectators, pronounces an oracle, reports a vision. Samuel runs to Eli, and Eli addresses Samuel. These are examples of simple activities nesting within the larger segment. As Beckerman writes:

> The concept of nesting is useful as long as the task we are examining is static. In conceiving work to be done or in remembering work already done, we can envision a totality—sewing, subdivided into segments. Clearly this is not how we experience segmentation in the theatre, where, as we encounter activity, we gain a sense of the rhythmic units through a process of accretion. Accretion is "the growing together of separate parts into a single whole." As we receive successive impressions of a presentation, we link them in coherent units and then add unit to unit by internalizing each as part of the unit before. Moreover, we absorb the segmental pattern of presentation kinesthetically rather than perceive it focally, that is, we absorb it with our muscles as well as our minds.[43]

As we have suggested, the arrangement of the activity in segments is determined largely by a selection and feedback process, which results in modes of presentation that create the communicative context for the playwright-actor-audience relationship. Within this context, when we view the scribe as creator of the Amos drama, the narrative (7:10–17) has an intrinsically valuable contribution to make to the vision sequence. Not only does this segment allow the scribe to be present in his own presentation (as narrator), but the variety the segment introduces into the vision sequence enhances the sense of conflict experienced by the spectators. The scale of the relationship between plot (action) and story is momentarily tipped toward story, layering the prophetic drama with an intensely personal moment of crisis for the prophet.

---

42. Beckerman, *Dynamics of Drama*, 42.
43. Ibid., 43.

This moment of crisis is played by the scribe, who becomes the prophet himself for his spectators: "I am no prophet, nor a prophet's son; but I am a herdsman, and a dresser of sycamore trees, and the LORD took me from following the flock, and the LORD said to me, 'Go, prophesy to my people Israel'" (7:14–15)

In the process of accretion that occurs throughout the development of the vision sequence (twice Amos persuades the Lord to withhold judgment, twice the Lord pronounces judgment based on what Amos sees, and finally the Lord stands only to deliver final judgment), the narrative humanizes Amos; it reminds the spectators that he was merely a shepherd obeying his God. Moller's comments about the function of Amaziah as the personification of the audience are not to be overlooked, particularly if the scribe is in the role of Amos. In the final vision sequence (9:1–4) when the scribe-as-actor enacts God's final judgment, the spectators become the people of Israel, who, like Amaziah, will be brought down by the falling pillars or struck down by God's sword. The scribe, having firmly established himself as Amos, will survive to play his drama again.

The role of the audience can be appreciated at the very end of the book as well. The concluding statement to the book has long caused debate among commentators:

> I will plant them upon their land,
> and they shall never again be plucked up
> out of the land that I have given them,
> says the LORD *your* God. (9:15)

It is certainly an unusual statement in Amos, both in its presentation of hope and in the style used to present that hope. These peculiarities have usually been resolved by claiming that the verse is a later addition to the book, the product of later redactional activity. Performance criticism encourages the reader to look at this ending to the book for its performative function.

Only here, in the ending verse to the book, is the reading or listening audience addressed directly. The appellation of "the LORD *your* God draws the audience into the performance. The story, whether read or acted out, is no longer about someone else somewhere else but is about the audience.

Although solely within the context of a reading audience, James Linville makes the point strikingly:

> The writers confront their readers with God's direct speech, which draws them into its own implied narrative. It is done subtly and brilliantly, with the final syllable, a final possessive. And so the book of Amos ends with a direct address to the reader, and, should the reader identify completely with Amos and the imperative to prophecy suggested in the visions and 3, 3–8, the reader closes with a prophetic promise to Israel.[44]

This concluding statement to the book signals the conclusion of several transformations. In the case of the scribe-as-performer and his ability to appropriate the power of the prophet through his creation and performance of the text, this final moment is critical. The scribe, speaking as God, turns from the drama of destruction to the drama of hope and salvation. No longer roaring from Zion, the Lord declares a new era. His final words, "says the LORD your God," are the gift of presentation. They constitute a personal exchange between presenter and spectator, both of whom have fully engaged with the reality of the drama.

CONCLUSION

The vision reports in the book of Amos exhibit an economy of action as well as a clear schematic relationship to an encompassing code that effectively lend themselves to the tools of dramatic analysis. Even more than prophetic dramas that require no reporting to be effective, the visions presuppose that they will be reported and so require a structure that unites act-image, act-scheme, and the surrounding literary code. Performance criticism makes plain the structure and movement of the vision reports in Amos. The five reports form a dramatic unity and use the surrounding narrative and oracles to enhance the dramatic action.

The application of performance criticism to the vision reports offers a challenge to the scholarly consensus that accepts a multilayered composition

44. Linville, "Visions and Voices," 42.

of the book. There is a unity to the visions and a clear rationale to their present placement within the book of Amos. When condensed and placed back-to-back, the dramatic visions flow naturally as a series of acts in a unified dramatic presentation. The strategic placement of the vision reports within the current structure of the text is an important feature that assists the development of the act-scheme of the visions. When left in its present literary structure, the interspersed oracles and narratives further develop the code and act-scheme of the visions and so form a coherent whole dramatized in the act-image. While recognizing the differences in form and vocabulary among the visions, there is an even greater unity in function and message. Even if composed in multiple layers, the current redaction of the visions has brought them into a unified whole that integrates well with the surrounding oracle and narrative material.

CHAPTER SEVEN

The Concluding Act

This book has demonstrated the use of performance criticism with application to the literature of the Bible. Performance criticism recognizes the remnants of oral performances in the literature of the Hebrew Bible and gives a conceptual framework for analyzing those performances. Performance criticism acknowledges that human discourse involves more than the exchange of ideas through the medium of language, but involves the engagement of the imagination as well. While sharing some characteristics of form criticism, tradition criticism, and narrative criticism, performance criticism differs from these other methodologies in that it focuses upon a performance mode of thought in an effort to capture the imaginative as well as cognitive aspect of human discourse.

Throughout the preceding chapters of this book, we have sought to develop some of the key concepts that are regularly applied to the event and occurrence of drama and theatre, molding them into a form applicable to the biblical text. The growing number of scholars who have recognized the dramatic aspects of the Hebrew prophets have led us to dig deeper and more systematically into the pages of the prophetic literature as a prospective location for the application of performance criticism. We have found that the pages of the Hebrew Bible, particularly the Hebrew prophets, constitute a rich field of study for performance criticism. We discovered that the imagination is regularly addressed in the prophets, and that the visual images presented through the words of the prophets come vibrantly alive when placed into an oral medium of human presentational discourse. In other words, the prophets communicated both cognitively and imaginatively, and both can still be found in the scribal appropriation of the prophetic traditions.

But our investigation into the Hebrew prophets led to a second interesting discovery. Not only do concepts commonly used in drama and performance have application to the Hebrew Bible, but the material of the Hebrew Bible has an important contribution to make to the investigation of the history of theatre. With few exceptions, the field of theatre history remains primarily focused on Western theatre history, beginning with the Greeks. The primary reason for this is the convenience of material evidence (extant plays, theatre structures, documents) that make a clear case for a literature-based theatre tradition. It is a welcome development that, in recent years, the theatres of Asia and Africa have been given considerably more attention by theatre historians, though still primarily through the lens of ritual and storytelling. Discussion of any notion of theatre preceding the Greeks, even when considering the multiple Pyramid Texts and Memphite Drama of the ancient Egyptians, is still dominated by the theory of ritual origins.[1] When other Near Eastern cultures are considered at all, it is generally in a subsidiary fashion next to the Egyptian material. For example, consider the following statement by Oscar Brockett and Franklin Hildy:

> By 3500 to 3000 B.C.E., cities had grown up in both Mesopotamia and Egypt, and by 3000 Egypt had formed an effective central government. For 2500 years thereafter, Egypt and the Near East were to be major centers of civilization. Forms of writing were devised and elaborate monuments were erected. Although Egypt and the Near East developed more or less simultaneously, . . . Egypt . . . was

1. See Oscar G. Brockett and Franklin J. Hildy, *History of Theatre* (9th ed.; Boston: Allyn & Bacon, 2003); as well as E. A. W. Budge, *Osiris and the Egyptian Resurrection* (2 vols.; New York: G. P. Putnam, 1911); Gerald F. Else, *The Origin and Early Form of Greek Tragedy* (Cambridge: Cambridge University Press, 1964); Theodor Gaster, *Thespis: Ritual, Myth, and Drama in the Ancient Near East* (New York: Henry Schuman, 1950); Benjamin Hunningher, *The Origin of the Theatre* (The Hague: M. Nithoff, 1955); and Jennifer Wise, *Dionysus Writes: The Invention of Theatre in Ancient Greece* (Ithaca, N.Y.: Cornell University Press, 1998).

> more stable than the Near East, where numerous empires (Sumerian, Babylonian, Hittite, Assyrian, Chaldean, Canaanite, and Persian) flourished and declined.[2]

In other words, Egypt has pride of place simply because of political continuity, not because of any dramatic or presentational consideration. All that aside, the Pyramid Texts are important. The continuing debate concerning them remains whether or not they were intended to be acted out. Though there are scholars who insist that these texts are dramas, "equally reputable scholars have denied that these texts were performed, pointing out that such nondramatic works as epic poems and the Bible also contain passages in dialogue and indications of action."[3] Certainly this denial becomes less convincing if it is shown that at least some of the biblical material is indeed within the dramatic stream. Vestiges of dramatic and performative material in the Hebrew Bible constitute an important witness to the origins of theatre tradition.

The question of the origins of theatre continues to be an active area of investigation for theatre historians. Is theatre somewhere between religious and secular ritual practice in its roots? Or, as we have suggested, are its roots somewhere in the imagination? As Eli Rozik points out, the thesis that theatre was generated by ritual[4] is fairly new and results from a nineteenth-century scholarly movement "with regard to the crucial role of the Church in the recreation of European theatre."[5] In both instances, traditional theatre

2. Brockett and Hildy, *History of Theatre*, 6–7.

3. Ibid., 7.

4. Other examples of works that explore this thesis include: Catherine Bell, *Ritual Theory, Ritual Practice* (Oxford: Oxford University Press, 1992); Bell, *Ritual: Perspectives and Dimensions* (Oxford: Oxford University Press, 1997); A. H. Blackman, "Myth and Ritual in Ancient Egypt," in S. H. Hooke, ed., *Myth and Ritual* (London: Oxford University Press, 1933), 15–39; Linda Christian, *Theatrum Mundi: The History of an Idea* (New York: Garland, 1987); George Cristea, "Pre-Theatre: Rock Paintings and Engravings in Central Sahara (Tassili n. Ajjer)," *Assaph—Studies in the Theatre* 7 (1991): 121–60; George Fredley and John A. Reeves, *A History of the Theatre* (New York: Crown, 1968); Phyllis Hartnoll, *A Concise History of the Theatre* (London: Thames & Hudson, 1971); Ernest T. Kirby, *Ur-Drama: The Origins of Theatre* (New York: New York University Press, 1975); and Eli Rozik, "The Common Roots of Dreams and Theatre," *Assaph—Studies in the Theatre* 7 (1991): 75–102.

5. Eli Rozik, *The Ritual Roots of Theatre: Rethinking Ritual and Other Theories of Origin* (Iowa City: University of Iowa Press, 2002), 3. Rozik also suggests a theory of theatre that relies heavily on the imagistic, or imaginative practices innate to the human being: "Instead of theories of origins, based on traces of ritual practices and/or beliefs in newly created forms, I suggest a theory of roots, based on the existential sources of theatre" (xi).

history and ritual origin theories, a methodological problem arises from the definition of terms: *ritual, drama,* and *theatre.* As Rozik points out, "Not only are scholars in disagreement on such definitions, but also, in most cases, these definitions are not even provided and must be extrapolated from the actual uses of these terms."[6]

Given the tendency to minimize the ancient Near East in the history of theatre, performance criticism of the Hebrew Bible has the potential to make a significant contribution to the study of the history of drama and theatre. Performance criticism makes a contribution to the history of theatre studies in two respects. First, the performance and dramatic repertoire of the Hebrew prophets must have been extensive.[7] There are indications that dramatic acts as well as spoken oracles were part and parcel of the cultural heritage of at least Iron Age Israel, contemporary with the New Kingdom of Egypt. This dramatic repertoire within the cultural stock of ancient Israel gives evidence of a well-developed presentational tradition.

Second, the literary tradition of the scribes that appropriated the prophetic performance also represents a step in the developing history of theatre. That scribal tradition is inexorably linked with cultural movements of the seventh century onward. The practices of the Assyrian Empire in the seventh century B.C.E. has had long lasting and unintended consequences. Ethnic relocation created an environment rich in cultural dialogue. Mixed with the later domination of the Babylonians and the cultural exile of the Israelites into Babylonia, a forced re-visioning of space and location was required. Jerusalem was no longer isolated on a hill but part of something much larger and bigger than the solitary kingdom of Judah. The literary tradition that became the Hebrew Bible was part of the re-visioning process. And that re-visioning incorporated the prophetic performance with a performance mode of thought that now could imagine the God of Judah on a much grander scale. This same Lord was God of the universe, not just of Judah. The Hebrew prophets used performative techniques and language in articulating their expanded vision of God.

---

6. Ibid., 3.

7. Compare the lists found in David Stacey, *Prophetic Drama in the Old Testament* (London: Epworth, 1990); A. van den Born, *Profetie Metterdaad* (Roermond: Maaseik, 1947); and A. W. Groenman, *Het Karakter van de Symbolische Handelingen der Oud-testamentlische Profeten* (Haarlem: H. D. Tjeenk Willink, 1942).

In some ways we have only scratched the surface of the layers of performance criticism that can be brought to bear on appropriate biblical texts. For example, in addition to the use of the performance categories of explicit and implicit activity, individual *stage speeches* can be identified within segments of activity. The stage speech is a specific type of theatrical activity that interacts with the overall action of the drama. Stage speeches, as opposed to narrative passages, are directed at bringing about change, effecting internal shifts, and creating confrontation.[8] Transitions from speech to speech imply actions of the mind that affect the physical reality of the individual speaking. As Beckerman points out, stage speeches reflect the forces of pressure and resistance that characters encounter as they pursue their projects. Stage speeches have taken many forms over the historical evolution of the theatre; monologues, soliloquies, messenger speeches, and debates are only a portion of the varieties of stage speeches known to actors and spectators alike. Deeper analysis of the oracles, visions, sermons, and doxologies of prophetic texts as stage speeches within the context of segmented dramatic action are certain to bring these texts to life in new and interesting ways.

The prophetic drama as an intensive mode of drama also has the potential for deeper and broader application. Intensive modes of drama are marked by late points of attack, causality, conflict, and a movement toward resolution.[9] Intensive modes of drama rely primarily on binary action, or two essential forces in conflict with one another.[10] Binary action can take the shape of both simple and complex patterns of action, sometimes within the same drama. Throughout theatre history, playwrights who make use of the binary structure of drama have done so with different degrees of sophistication and efficiency. The process of comparing one prophetic text to another for variations in binary structure would be a very useful endeavor. The historical evidence of binary action is extensive and appears also to be the dominant form of action in the prophetic drama. However, even binary action can develop into triangular planes of performance, or performance within performance.

8. Bernard Beckerman, *Theatrical Presentation: Performer, Audience, and Act* (ed. Gloria Brim Beckerman and William Coco; New York: Routledge, 1990), 233.

9. See the discussion in chapter 3 of the concept of intensive mode of drama.

10. Beckerman, *Theatrical Presentation*, 176.

These concepts offer rich territory for further exploration, particularly in relationship to the scribal performance of the prophetic text and the communal audience the scribes sought to sustain. "Whatever anyone wishes to communicate theatrically," says Beckerman, "it has to be done through the performer."[11] Knowing what we know about the scribe as performer, we have only begun to explore the theatre of the prophet and scribe.

Finally, in the theatre, when something is intended for performance, there is always a process of orchestration that brings the performance to fruition. This process can include multiple players, or just a few. In the modern theatre, we have come to rely on writers, directors, designers, choreographers, technicians, and a variety of stage crews to orchestrate the performance. In the case of prophetic dramas, we need to carefully examine the complex interplay between scribe, prophet, and cultural context. "Since the writer is usually the inventor of the fiction that the actor plays, it is tempting to give him or her primacy. From the point of view of actual practice, this is too simple a proposition, for in the shaping of an actor's performance we can discern three distinct planes of form."[12] Beckerman identifies these three planes of form as: the language of forms the art of presentation can accommodate (the possible kind of presentation that can be generated), the cultural forms that dominate any given period, and the individual expressions of the language of forms (the performing process that generally precedes and shapes the work of the creator of a text.)[13] Through exploration of some aspects of each of these planes, a broader and richer reading will arise from the biblical texts.

It is likely that performance criticism and a performance mode of thought will find application throughout the Hebrew Bible. Already, the book of Zephaniah has been identified as a "prophetic drama,"[14] and it seems promising that a performance criticism could be applied beneficially to that part of

11. Ibid., 185.

12. Ibid., 186.

13. Ibid., 187.

14. See Paul House, *Zephaniah: A Prophetic Drama* (Journal for the Study of the Old Testament: Supplement Series 69; Sheffield: Sheffield Academic Press, 1989).

15. James Crenshaw writes, "The abundance of imperatives, and thus the frequency of direct address, marks the urgency of Joel's message and suggests oral presentation." Crenshaw, *Joel* (New York: Doubleday, 1995), 39.

the Book of the Twelve. Parallels between Amos and Joel[15] and similar material shared with Isaiah[16] may indicate that these prophetic books as well may yield fresh insights when examined by performance criticism. Form critics have long recognized that many, if not all, of the psalms were sung in public performances of the cult or the court.[17] As such, they too can rightly be considered scripts and so open to an examination of a performance mode of thought. Likewise, the Song of the Sea and Miriam's Song, both in Exodus, and of course the Song of Songs[18] seem ripe for the application of performance criticism. Also, the epics of the Pentateuch, particularly those parts identified by source critics as J, may be a rich field of examination for performance criticism.[19] The creation materials, both the Genesis accounts and remnants found in the prophets, seem to readily engage the reader both cognitively and imaginatively and so lend themselves to performance criticism.[20]

Now it falls to explore further. The conceptual tools of performance criticism that we have introduced in this book must be refined, and more tools wait to be added. The selection and improvement of those tools will come with use. In the long run, some will be found to be of little help, but others will prove to be of significant value in delving into the Hebrew Bible.

---

16. See Klaus Baltzer, *Deutero Isaiah* (Minneapolis: Fortress, 2001).

17. See William Brown, *Seeing the Psalms: A Theology of Metaphor* (Louisville, Ky.: Westminster John Knox, 2002), as well as some of the more established commentaries: Arthur Weiser, *The Psalms* (trans. Herbert Hartwell; Old Testament Library; Philadelphia: Westminster, 1962); Hans Joachim Kraus, *Psalms 1–59* (trans. Hilton Oswald; Minneapolis: Augsburg, 1988); Kraus, *Psalms 60–150* (trans. Hilton Oswald; Minneapolis: Augsburg, 1989); Sigmund Mowinckle, *The Psalms in Israel's Worship* (2 vols.; trans. D. Ap-Thomas; New York: Abingdon, 1962); and J. Day, *Psalms* (Sheffield: Sheffield Academic Press, 1990).

18. See Marvin Pope, *Song of Songs* (New York: Doubleday, 1977).

19. See Michael Fishbane, *Text and Texture* (New York: Schocken, 1979).

20. See Howard Wallace, *The Eden Narrative* (Atlanta: Scholars Press, 1985).

GLOSSARY

This glossary is a compendium of terms and concepts meant to assist the reader with the application of performance criticism to additional biblical texts. References are given to credit sources from which some of the concepts were synthesized.

Act. A standard division of dramatic literature. Plays/scripts are generally divided into acts according to the prevailing practice of a given historical period. The act structure is also a way of dividing a script's activity into larger units, with scenes or segments as the smaller units of activity. In a theatrical rather than dramatic context, an act describes the presentation given by a performer. For example, a juggler may juggle five or six different kinds of objects as part of his act.

Act-image. The result of the actual activity (what the actor does) and the virtual activity (what the character does). In the performance of a drama, it is the appearance of that which is perceived by the spectator. (Beckerman, *Dynamics of Drama*)

Act-scheme. The structural organization of the drama's activity. Historically, dramatic structure is governed by a process of selection and feedback, resulting in recognizable literary and performance structures shared by both performers and spectators. It is the pattern of organization that facilitates the presentation of the drama. (Beckerman, *Dynamics of Drama*)

Action. Dramatic activity has a contradictory nature. It arouses interest for what is perceptible in the here and now but also is a representation of, or window into, imagined life. Action is the result of these two planes of reality simultaneously evoked by the interplay between stage activity and imagined act. In essence, the action is what is revealed by actors engaged in the living out of the dramatic activity. (Beckerman, *Dynamics of Drama*)

Active Segment. A unit of dramatic activity in which confrontation and rising tension move the drama toward a specific goal. (Beckerman, *Dynamics of Drama.*)

Actor. The agent of presentation in the drama. The actor is always engaged in a double effort: the demonstration of actual skill and the portrayal of virtual existence. (Beckerman, *Theatrical Presentation*)

Audience. An essential ingredient in performance. If there is no audience, there is no theatre or drama. Performance is heightened by the very fact that it is on display for an audience. The audience is the target of the drama's inner life. For the drama to be realized in performance, something must be held between the performers and spectators: an interplay that requires both as participants. (Beckerman, *Theatrical Presentation; Dynamics of Drama*)

Audience response. A critical element in both the selection and feedback process that forms and shapes the drama, but also within the life of the drama itself. Since the audience is the ultimate target for the actors' energies (pursuing the characters' projects in order to make the inner life of the drama appear for the spectators), the various ways an audience provides feedback to the actor(s) is critical to sustaining the shared virtual world of the drama. Following a performance, there is also the memorial response of the audience, which can, and usually does, vary significantly from the response during the performance.

Character. The medium of the drama is human presence, not just language, or even a combination of thought and diction (Aristotle). In performance terms, character is the *result* of a human presence (actor) engaged in portraying a virtual existence. Character appears as a result of an actor's pursuit of the character's project. More than the Aristotelian notion of "good and/or bad" qualities, in performance terms, character emerges from the pursuit of a project. (Beckerman, *Dynamics of Drama*)

Closed performance. According to De Marinis, closed performances anticipate an audience with certain competencies in relationship to the content and the nature of the performance. Closed performances rely on audience recognition, shared history, mythology, or background of cultural experience. In closed performances there is a transparent relationship between the audience the work is intended for (ideal) and the actual audience participating in the performance experience.

Communal audience. A group of spectators whose total social experience is in harmony with the presenters. Presenters and audience share nearly identical values, thoughts, and language. A communal audience brings expectations to the performance that generally must be met by the performance in order to sustain the communal audience both during and after the performance. For the scribe as both author and performer of the prophetic text, building and sustaining a communal audience would have been critical. (Beckerman, *Dynamics of Drama*)

Conceptional profile of discourse. A concept introduced by Oesterreicher, corresponding closely to the notions of closed performance and communal audience. The profile demonstrates how the conditions of communication come together to create a communicative context, conforming to preexisting traditions of discourse with patterns implicitly agreed upon by all participants.

Context of expectation. According to Beckerman, every age finds certain recurrent presentational activities satisfying. Through the interaction of performers and spectators over time, a representative collection of activities is amassed that becomes available to later writers and performers. From the resulting framework of socioaesthetic practices, artists can select materials and performance structures from a context of expectation. In this way, a performance tradition emerges that is sustained and changed over time through the selection and feedback process that occurs during performance. (Beckerman, *Dynamics of Drama; Theatrical Presentation*)

Contrast. Varying degrees between the effort and the expected result of characters' projects. When two or more characters are pursuing projects that have different trajectories, they are in contrast to one another. This contrast is a crucial ingredient in developing the tension and conflict of the drama. Contrast also helps to establish variety for the spectator, a component essential to maintaining the spectator's attention. (Beckerman, *Dynamics of Drama*)

Crux. Different from the traditional Aristotelian notion of crisis, the concept of crux places more emphasis on the flow of the drama's action. Crisis is traditionally defined in terms of critical decision moments for characters. A crux is more focused on the accumulative effect of dramatic activity and can be associated both with extreme moments of intensification and with moments of decreasing intensity. A crux, from segment to segment, may or may not be associated with a moment of decision for a character. (Beckerman, *Dynamics of Drama*)

Decresence. The decline of tension following a period of intensification in the drama. Related to crux, this is the moment when the crux of the drama transitions into a movement away from intensification. This can be a sustained or a brief period, depending on the nature of the drama. (Beckerman, *Dynamics of Drama*)

Dialectical element of performance. According to Beckerman, this is the nothing we respond to during performance. It is the dialectical exchange between the performance, the space and time of the performance, and the witnesses to the performance. Dramas that are primarily dialectical in nature are always moving toward an imagined future, the dialectical process of becoming. (Beckerman, *Dynamics of Drama; Theatrical Presentation*)

Drama. Occurs when one or more human beings isolated in time and/or space present themselves in imagined acts to another or others. (Beckerman, *Dynamics of Drama; Theatrical Presentation*)

Dramaturgy: According to De Marinis, the set of techniques or theories governing the composition of a theatrical text.

Explicit activity. Everything the script and performance present visually and aurally to the spectator. The activities of the characters (e.g., walking, talking, fighting, begging, pleading, praying, threatening), are all part of the *something* a performance gives us. (Beckerman, *Dynamics of Drama*)

Horizon of expectations. Similar to Beckerman's notion of the foreground/background nature of the drama, this is a concept from the work of Hans Robert Jauss concerning the empirical disposition of readers/audience when they encounter a text. The horizon of expectations of the readers/audience is based on the norms of the genre, the implicit relationship to other familiar work, and opposition between fiction and reality.

Iconic element of performance. According to Beckerman, this is what a performance gives the audience to respond to, that which is offered for display. Sound, color, movement—all of these are part of what is given to the audience. Dramas that are primarily iconic in nature (e.g., parades, shows of glorification) emphasize the static nature of what is, rather than the dialectical process of becoming. (Beckerman, *Theatrical Presentation*)

Imagined act. The inner life of the drama as revealed through performance. The imagined act is the culmination of the interaction between performer(s), spectators, and the realized scheme of the drama. (Beckerman, *Dynamics of Drama*)

Implicit activity. The *how* of the explicit activity. The simplest activity can be performed in any number of ways. For example, "Samuel goes to Eli." *How* does he go? Quickly, hesitantly, reluctantly? The patterns of explicit activity, along with other clues in the script/text, provide the framework for the interpretive process of determining the implicit nature of that activity. (Beckerman, *Dynamics of Drama*)

Inner life of the drama. What the presentation of the drama seeks to reveal or make appear. Through the living out of the action of the drama by actors pursuing the projects of characters, an inner life is revealed—not the inner life of the actor, but of the character and the path of action the character is part of. The inner life of the drama is the invisible made visible through the act of presentation. The inner life of the drama is where the performers and spectators connect. (Beckerman, *Dynamics of Drama*)

Intensive mode of drama. This occurs when the moment of time a character has been forced into results from a progression of pressures that place the character in an unmaneuverable position. (Beckerman, *Dynamics of Drama*).

Intensity and velocity. Features of dramatic activity as it unfolds in segments. Intensity refers to the degree of conflict and tension associated with activity, while velocity refers to the pace of that activity. For example, God's punishment in the prophetic dramas can be swift, slow, painful, immediate, torturous, or long-suffering. (Beckerman, *Dynamics of Drama*)

Intention. Part of a character's project. Two characters may share the same intention to become wealthy. One character may intend to do this by hard work and frugal living, while another character may intend to do this by spending his entire paycheck on lottery tickets. The contrast between their intentions becomes part of the path of the drama's action. (Beckerman, *Dynamics of Drama; Theatrical Presentation*)

Linguistic conception. An analytical concept that describes the oral versus literary origin of a communication.

Linguistic medium. The oral versus literary medium in which a communication takes place.

Medium transferability. The ability of the conceptional profile of a communication to transfer to a second medium without affecting the conceptual content of the communication.

Mimesis. According to Bert States, mimesis in its original Aristotelian sense is performance in which the performers are not themselves, and *not not* themselves.

Model spectator. A hypothetical construct developed by De Marinis based on Eco's *model reader*. De Marinis developed this concept to show how a performance anticipates a certain type of spectator and therefore a certain type of reception.

Mouvance. A concept formulated to describe textual mobility in medieval texts when the creation of a work is the result of a communal process rather than an individual act of literary production.

Open performance. According to De Marinis, open performances anticipate a receiver who is not too clearly defined in terms of the cultural, historical, and social context of the performance.

Performance arena. The physical space that contains the boundaries of the performance. The performance arena can be, and often is, created as part of the performance. It is the spatial aspect of the spatiotemporal nature of the drama.

Performance mode of thought. The peculiar type of orality still evidenced in the prophetic literature of the Hebrew Bible. This is a way of thinking that engages both the cognitive and the imaginative aspects of thought to conceive of reality not in propositions but in actions and being. Similar to the notion of a dramatic imagination, it is the shared imaginative space of performance where both actors and spectators are transformed.

Performance space-time. Time and space are the axes upon which the drama moves, or occurs. Performance space-time occurs within the framework of real space-time, but simultaneously transcends real space-time through the creation of the imagined world of the drama.

Performance text. According to De Marinis, the techniques or theories governing the composition of a performance. This includes the signs, expressive means, and actions that can be "read" by spectators.

Plot. Usually recognized as the sequence of events in a drama, or the discrete units of action that lead up to a play's climax. The concept of plot has limited use when dealing with aspects of performance because plot is generally not concerned with the dynamics within any given segment of activity or action, particularly as those elements are made to appear by the performance itself.

Potential theatre. A term introduced by Shimon Levy in *The Bible as Theatre* describing passages of the Bible that contain characteristics common to theatre and ritual. As Levy suggests, the potential theatre rests on the notion that certain sections of the Bible could be easily translated into theatrical performances.

Precipitating context. In a dramatic segment, the precipitating context is usually provided by the preceding segment. However, the primary content is the human being in defined space and time *engaged* in an imagined act. The precipitating context also includes background information shared by performers and spectators such as legend, mythology, and other socially and culturally shared information. (Beckerman, *Dynamics of Drama*)

Presentation. Another word for performance, presentation is the umbrella term for theatre, drama, and all other socioaesthetic practices through which human beings present themselves to one another.

Project. A combination of a character's intention and motivation. A character's project moves along certain trajectories, changing and adapting based on the types of resistance a character meets in the course of the drama.

More than simply what a character wants, the project also includes all the ways in which a character seeks to achieve desired goals. (Beckerman, *Dynamics of Drama*)

Random audience. A loose collection of individuals assembled randomly to witness a presentation. Unlike the communal audience, the random audience is not a group of people whose total social experience is at one with the presenters. (Beckerman, *Dynamics of Drama*)

Real space-time. The space-time experienced as part of everyday reality.

Resistance. The character experiences resistance to his project that is actual or potential. Resistance that is foreseen and unforeseen establishes the conflict in drama. How characters deal with this resistance establishes the variations in intensity expected by the audience. (Beckerman, *Dynamics of Drama*)

Rhythm of involvement. Spectators are only capable of certain degrees of focus of attention during a performance. The variety and intensity of the drama, along with the skill of the performer, creates a rhythm of involvement for the spectator. The rhythm of involvement can also be affected by the changing role of the spectator in the course of the drama.

Schematic activity. A sequence of perceptible signs created by the performer. These signs are visual and/or auditory. The schematic emerges from the presentational idea that forms the core of the act itself. The activity must then be appropriate to the idea of the presentation. (Beckerman, *Dynamics of Drama; Theatrical Presentation*)

Script. The performance term for a dramatic (literary) text. A script does not contain everything a performer needs. In fact, it is the script that needs the performer in order to be lived in the space-time of the drama.

Segment. The basic performative unit of the drama. The segment consists of the schematic activity that must be enacted by the performer. Segments are the basic temporal units of the performance and relate to each other in more than simple linear, causal connections. All forms of theatrical and dramatic presentation are made up of segments. (Beckerman, *Dynamics of Drama*)

Segmented dramatic activity. A unit of activity that contains the schematic activity of the imagined act of the drama. Segmented dramatic activity is distinct from segmented theatrical activity because of the imagined act. It is the difference between a juggler or tightrope walker and an actor engaged in the imaginary world of the drama. (Beckerman, *Dynamics of Drama*)

Spectator. The cocreator of the theatrical or dramatic experience. Since theatre and drama only occur when presented to another or others, the spectator is both observer and participant in the experience. In the case of the drama, the imagined act must be realized between the performers and the spectators. It is the spectator for whom the inner life of the drama is revealed.

Stage speech. A theatrical activity, interacting with action, bringing about changes, effecting internal shifts, and forcing confrontations. (Beckerman, *Dynamics of Drama*).

Tension. When there is evident contrast between a character's project and the resistance experienced by the character, tension emerges. It is both actual and imaginative: that which we can see, and that which we sense. (Beckerman, *Dynamics of Drama; Theatrical Presentation*)

Theatre. Theatre occurs when one or more human beings, isolated in time and/or space, present themselves to another or others. Theatre is the larger framework for acts of presentation. Drama is a form or subset of theatre. (Beckerman, *Dynamics of Drama*)

Theatrical activity. The full range of motion possible that creates what is perceived by the audience. Theatrical activity is skill based and is rooted in the actual activity the performer engages in. (Beckerman, *Dynamics of Drama; Theatrical Presentation*)

Vector. A sense of where a drama's contrasting elements are pointing; a framework for the future within which the characters' tasks are performed. It is defined by the performer and the performing situation. (Beckerman, *Dynamics of Drama*)

Willing suspension of disbelief. Coined by Samuel Taylor Coleridge in the nineteenth century. Though an audience knows the actor is engaged in the creation of an illusory world, they enter that world willingly in search of both reality and truth.

BIBLIOGRAPHY

Anderson, Robert. "Was Isaiah a Scribe?" *Journal of Biblical Literature* 69 (1960): 57–58.

Aristotle. *Aristotle's Poetics*. Translated by S. H. Butcher. New York: Hill & Wang, 1994.

Auld, A. "Prophets through the Looking Glass: Between Writings and Moses." *Journal for the Study of the Old Testament* 27 (1983): 3–23.

Bakker, Egbert, and Ahuvia Kahane. *Written Voices, Spoken Signs*. Cambridge, Mass.: Harvard University Press, 1977.

Baltzer, Klaus. *Deutero Isaiah*. Minneapolis: Fortress, 2001.

Barstad, Hans. "No Prophets? Recent Developments in Biblical Prophecy Research and Ancient Near Eastern Prophecy." *Journal for the Study of the Old Testament* 57 (1993): 39–60.

———. *The Religious Polemics of Amos: Studies in the Preaching of Amos* 2. Leiden: Brill, 1984.

Barton, John. *Oracles of God*. Oxford: Oxford University Press, 1986.

Bauman, Richard. *Verbal Art as Performance*. Prospect Heights, Ill.: Waveland, 1977.

———. *The Written Word: Literacy in Transition*. Oxford: Oxford University Press, 1986.

Beckerman, Bernard. *Dynamics of Drama: Theory and Method of Analysis*. New York: Drama Book Specialists, 1979.

———. *Theatrical Presentation: Performer, Audience, and Act*. Edited by Gloria Brim Beckerman and William Coco. New York: Routledge, 1990.

Bell, Catherine. *Ritual: Perspectives and Dimensions*. Oxford: Oxford University Press, 1997.

———. *Ritual Theory, Ritual Practice*. Oxford: Oxford University Press, 1992.

Ben Zvi, Ehud. "Studying Prophetic Texts against Their Original Back-Grounds: Pre-Ordained Scripts and Alternative Horizons of Research." Pages 125–35 in *Prophets and Paradigms: Essays in Honor of Gene M. Tucker*. Edited by S. Reid. Journal for the Study of the Old Testament: Supplement Series 229. Sheffield: Sheffield Academic Press, 1996.

Ben Zvi, Ehud, and Michael Floyd. "Introduction: Writings, Speeches, and the Prophetic Books—Setting an Agenda." Pages 1–30 in *Writings and Speech in Israelite and Ancient Near Eastern Prophecy*. Edited by Ehud Ben Zvi and Michael Floyd. Atlanta: Society of Biblical Literature, 2000.

———. *Writings and Speech in Israelite and Ancient Near Eastern Prophecy*. Atlanta: Society of Biblical Literature, 2000.

Blackman, A. H. "Myth and Ritual in Ancient Egypt." Pages 15–39 in *Myth and Ritual*. Edited by S. H. Hooke. London: Oxford University Press, 1933.

Blenkinsopp, Joseph. *A History of Prophecy in Israel*. Louisville, Ky.: Westminster John Knox, 1996.

Bovati, Pietro, and Roland Maynet. *Le livre du prophete Amos*. Rhetorique biblique 3. Paris: Cerf, 1994.

Bowman, A. K., and Greg Woolf, eds. *Literacy and Power in the Ancient World*. Cambridge: Cambridge University Press, 1994.

Brenner, A. *The Song of Songs*. Sheffield: Sheffield Academic Press, 1989.

Brockett, Oscar G., and Franklin J. Hildy. *History of Theatre*. 9th ed. Boston: Allyn & Bacon, 2003.

Brown, William. *Seeing the Psalms: A Theology of Metaphor*. Louisville, Ky.: Westminster John Knox, 2002.

Brueggemann, Walter. "Amos IV 4–13 and Israel's Covenant Worship." *Vetus Testamentum* 15 (1965): 1–15.

Budde, K. "Zur Geschichte des Buches Amos." Pages 63–77 in *Studien zur semitischen Philologie und Religionsgeschichte: Julius Wellhausen zum siebzigsten Geburtstag*.

Beihefte zur Zeitschrift für die alttestamentliche Wissenschaft 27. Giessen: Topelmann, 1914.

Budge, E. A. W. *Osiris and the Egyptian Resurrection.* 2 vols. New York: G. P. Putnam, 1911.

Camp, Claudia. "The Female Sage in Ancient Israel and in the Biblical Wisdom Literature." Pages 185–204 in *The Sage in Israel and the Ancient Near East.* Edited by John Gammie and Leo Perdue. Winona Lake, Ind.: Eisenbrauns, 1990.

Carlson, Marvin. *Performance: A Critical Introduction.* New York: Routledge, 2003.

———. "Theatre Audiences and the Reading of the Performance." Pages 82–98 in *Interpreting the Theatrical Past: Essays in the Historiography of Performance.* Edited by Thomas Postlewait and Bruce McConachie. Iowa City: University of Iowa Press, 1991.

———. *Theories of the Theatre: A Historical and Critical Survey from the Greeks to the Present.* Ithaca, N.Y.: Cornell University Press, 1984.

Carroll R., M. Daniel. *Amos: The Prophet and His Oracles.* Louisville, Ky.: Westminster John Knox, 2002.

Chafe, Wallace, and Jane Danielewicz. "Properties of Spoken and Written Language." Pages 83–112 in *Comprehending Oral and Written Language.* Edited by Rosiland Horowitz and S. Samuels. New York: Academic Press, 1987.

Christian, Linda. *Theatrum Mundi: The History of an Idea.* New York: Garland, 1987.

Clements, Ronald. "Max Weber, Charisma, and Biblical Prophecy." Pages 89–108 in *Prophecy and Prophets: The Diversity of Contemporary Issues in Scholarship.* Edited by Y. Gitay. Semeia Studies. Atlanta: Scholars Press, 1997.

Conrad, E. "The End of Prophecy and the Appearance of Angels: Messengers in the Book of the Twelve." *Journal for the Study of the Old Testament* 73 (1997): 65–79.

Coote, Robert. *Amos among the Prophets: Composition and Theology.* Philadelphia: Fortress, 1981.

Cramer, K. *Amos—Versuch einer theologischen Interpretation.* Beiträge zur Wissenschaft vom Alten und Neuen Testamant 15. Stuttgart: Kohlhammer, 1930.

Crenshaw, James. *Education in Ancient Israel.* New York: Doubleday, 1998.

———. *Hymnic Affirmation of Divine Justice: The Doxologies of Amos and Related Texts in the Old Testament*. Missoula, Mont.: Published by Scholars Press for the Society of Biblical Literature, 1975.

———. *Joel*. New York: Doubleday, 1995.

———. "Transmitting Prophecy across Generations." Pages 31–44 in *Writings and Speech in Israelite and Ancient Near Eastern Prophecy*. Edited by Ehud Ben Zvi and Michael Floyd. Atlanta: Society of Biblical Literature, 2000.

Cristea, George. "Pre-Theatre: Rock Paintings and Engravings in Central Sahara (Tassili n. Ajjer)." *Assaph—Studies in the Theatre* 7 (1991): 121–60.

Culley, Robert. "Orality and Writtenness in the Prophetic Texts." Pages 45–64 in *Writings and Speech in Israelite and Ancient Near Eastern Prophecy*. Edited by Ehud Ben Zvi and Michael Floyd. Atlanta: Society of Biblical Literature, 2000.

Davies, Philip. "The Audiences of Prophetic Scrolls: Some Suggestions." Pages 48–60 in *Prophets and Paradigms: Essays in Honor of Gene M. Tucker*. Edited by S. Reid. Journal for the Study of the Old Testament: Supplement Series 229. Sheffield: Sheffield Academic Press, 1996.

———. "The Jewish Scriptural Canon in Cultural Perspective." Pages 36–52 in *The Canon Debate*. Edited by Lee Martin McDonald and James Sanders. Peabody, Mass.: Hendrickson, 2002.

———. "Pen of Iron, Point of Diamond." Pages 65–82 in *Writers and Speech in Israelite and Ancient Near Eastern Prophecy*. Edited by Ehud Ben Zvi and Michael Floyd. Atlanta: Society of Biblical Literature, 2000.

———. *Scribes and Schools: The Canonization of the Hebrew Scriptures*. Louisville, Ky.: Westminster John Knox, 1998.

Day, J. *Psalms*. Sheffield: Sheffield Academic Press, 1990.

De Marinis, Marco. "Dramaturgy of the Spectator." *Drama Review* 31, no. 2 (Summer 1987): 100–114.

Deist, Ferdinand. "The Prophets: Are We Heading for a Paradigm Shift?" Pages 582–99 in *This Place Is Too Small for Us: The Israelite Prophets in Recent Scholarship*. Edited by R. Gordon. Winona Lake, Ind.: Eisenbrauns, 1995.

Doane, A. "The Ethnography of Scribal Writing and Anglo-Saxon Poetry: Scribe as Performer." *Oral Tradition* 9 (1994): 420–39.

Dorsey, David. "Literary Architecture and Aural Structuring Techniques in Amos." *Biblica* 73 (1992): 305–30.

Douglas, Mary. *Purity and Danger*. London: Routledge & Kegan Paul, 1966.

Dufrenne, Mikel. *The Phenomenology of Aesthetic Experience*. Translated by Edward

S. Casey et al. Evanston, Ill.: Northwestern University Press, 1993.

Dukore, Bernard. *Dramatic Theory and Criticism: Greeks to Grotowski*. New York: Holt, Rinehart & Winston, 1974.

Eco, Umberto. *The Role of the Reader*. Bloomington: Indiana University Press, 1979.

Else, Gerald F. *The Origin and Early Form of Greek Tragedy*. Cambridge: Cambridge University Press, 1964.

Eslinger, L. "The Education of Amos." *Hebrew Annual Review* 11 (1987): 35–57.

Esslin, Martin. *An Anatomy of Drama*. New York: Hill & Wang, 1976.

Fergusson, Francis. *The Idea of Theatre*. New York: Doubleday Anchor, 1994.

———. Introductory essay. Pages 2–44 in *Aristotle's Poetics*. New York: Hill & Wang, 1961.

Fishbane, Michael. *Text and Texture*. New York: Schocken Books, 1979.

Floyd, Michael. "'Write the Revelation!' (Hab 2:2): Re-imagining the Cultural History of Prophecy." Pages 103–43 in *Writings and Speech in Israelite and Ancient Near Eastern Prophecy*. Edited by Ehud Ben Zvi and Michael Floyd. Atlanta: Society of Biblical Literature, 2000.

Fohrer, Georg. *History of Israelite Religion* Translated by David Green. Nashville: Abingdon, 1972.

Fohrer, Georg, and Ernst Sellin. *Introduction to the Old Testament.*Translated by David Green. Nashville: Abingdon, 1968.

Fontaine, Carole. *Smooth Words: Women, Proverbs, and Performance in Biblical Wisdom*. London: Sheffield Academic Press, 2002.

Fredley, George, and John A. Reeves. *A History of the Theatre*. New York: Crown, 1968.

Gaster, Theodor. *Thespis: Ritual, Myth, and Drama in the Ancient Near East*. New York: Henry Schuman, 1950.

Giles, Terry. "A Note on the Vocation of Amos in 7:14." *Journal of Biblical Literature* 111 (Winter 1992): 690–92.

Gittlen, Barry. *Sacred Time, Sacred Place: Archaeology and the Religion of Israel*. Winona Lake, Ind.: Eisenbrauns, 2002.

Goody, Jack. *The Domestication of the Savage Mind*. Cambridge: Cambridge University Press, 1977.

Gordon, Robert. "Present Trends and Future Directions." Pages 600–605 in *This Place Is Too Small for Us: The Israelite Prophets in Recent Scholarship*. Edited by

R. Gordon. Winona Lake, Ind.: Eisenbrauns, 1995.

Gottwald, Norman. "Ideology and Ideologies in Israelite Prophecy." Pages 136–49 in *Prophets and Paradigms: Essays in Honor of Gene M. Tucker*. Edited by S. Reid. Journal for the Study of the Old Testament: Supplement Series 229. Sheffield: Sheffield Academic Press, 1996.

Groenman, Albertus W. *Het Karakter van de Symbolische Handelingen der Oud-Testamentlische Profeten*. Haarlem: H. D. Tjeenk Willink, 1942.

Gunkel, Hermann. "The Israelite Prophecy from the Time of Amos." Pages 136–49 in *Twentieth Century Theology in the Making*. Edited J. Pelikan. Translated by R. Wilson. Vol. 1, *Themes of Biblical Theology*. New York: Harper & Row, 1969.

Halliday, Michael. "Spoken and Written Modes of Meaning." Pages 55–82 in *Comprehending Oral and Written Language*. Edited by Rosiland Horowitz and S. Samuels. New York: Academic Press, 1987.

Harper, William R. *A Critical and Exegetical Commentary on Hosea and Amos*. Edinburgh: T&T Clark, 1905.

Hartnoll, Phyllis. *A Concise History of the Theatre*. London: Thames & Hudson, 1971.

Hasel, Gerhard. *Understanding the Book of Amos*. Grand Rapids: Eerdmans, 1991.

Havelock, E. A. "The Coming of Literate Communication to Western Civilization." *Journal of Communication* 30 (1980): 90–98.

———. *Origins of Western Literacy*. Toronto: Ontario Institute for the Study of Education, 1976.

Hayes, John. *Amos, the Eighth-Century Prophet: His Time and His Preaching*. Nashville: Abingdon, 1988.

Herder, J. *The Spirit of Hebrew Poetry*. 2 vols. Translated by J. Marsh. Burlington, Vt.: Edwin Smith Publishers, 1833.

Heschel, Abraham. *The Prophets*. New York: Harper & Row, 1962.

Holscher, G. *Die Propheten: Untersuchungen zur Religionsgeschichte Israels*. Leipzig: Hinrich, 1914.

Horowitz, Rosiland, and S. Jay Samuels. *Comprehending Oral and Written Language*. New York: Academic Press, 1987.

Horst, F. "Die Doxologien im Amosbuch." *Zeitschrift für die alttestamentliche Wissenschaft* 47 (1929): 45–54.

House, Paul. *Zephaniah: A Prophetic Drama*. Journal for the Study of the Old

Testament: Supplement Series 69. Sheffield: Sheffield Academic Press, 1989.

Humphry, J. *Literacy in the Roman World.* Ann Arbor, Mich.: University Press, 1991.

Hunninger, Benjamin. *The Origin of Theatre.* The Hague: M. Nithoff, 1955.

Jauss, Hans Robert. *Toward an Aesthetic of Reception.* Trans. Timothy Bahti. Minneapolis: University of Minnesota Press, 1982.

Jeremias, Jorg. *The Book of Amos.* Translated by Douglas Scott. Old Testament Library. Louisville, Ky.: Westminster John Knox, 1998.

King, Philip. *Amos, Hosea, Micah: An Archaeological Commentary.* Philadelphia: Westminster, 1988.

Kirby, Ernest T. *Ur-Drama: The Origins of Theatre.* New York: New York University Press, 1975.

Koch, K. "Die Rolle der hymnischen Abschnitte in der Komposition des Amos-Buches." *Zeitschrift für die alttestamentliche Wissenschaft* 86 (1974): 504–37.

Kraus, Hans Joachim. *Psalms 1–59.* Translated by Hilton Oswald. Minneapolis: Augsburg, 1988.

———. *Psalms 60–150.* Translated by Hilton Oswald. Minneapolis: Augsburg, 1989.

Kreiman, Gabriel, Christof Koch, and Itzhak Fried. "Imagery Neurons in the Human Brain." *Nature* 408 (2000): 357–61.

Lang, Bernard. *Anthropological Approaches to the Old Testament.* Philadelphia: Fortress, 1985.

———. *Monotheism and the Prophetic Minority.* Sheffield: Almond, 1983.

———. "Street Theater: Raising the Dead and the Zoroastrian Connection in Ezekiel's Prophecy." Pages 297–316 in *Ezekiel and His Book.* Edited by J. Lust. Bibliotheca ephemeridum theologicarum lovaniensium 74. Leuven: Peeters, 1986.

Lausberg, Heinrich. *Romanische Sprachwissenschaft.* Vol. 1. Berlin: De Gruyter, 1969.

Levy, Shimon. *The Bible as Theatre.* Portland: Sussex Academic Press, 2002.

Lindblom, J. *Prophecy in Ancient Israel.* Philadelphia: Fortress, 1962.

Linville, James. "'Amos among the Dead Prophet's Society': Re-reading the Lion's Roar." *Journal for the Study of the Old Testament* 90 (2000): 55–77.

———. "Visions and Voices: Amos 7–9." *Biblica* 80 (1999): 22–42.

Long, Burke. "Reports of Visions among the Prophets." *Journal of Biblical Literature* 95 (1976): 359–60.

Lord, A. B. *Singer of Tales.* New York: Atheneum, 1965.

Lowth, R. *Lectures on the Sacred Poetry of the Hebrews.* Translated by G. Gregory. London: Thomes Tegg & Son, 1835.

Lyons, John. *Language and Linguistics.* Cambridge: Cambridge University Press, 1981.

Mays, James. *Amos.* Philadelphia: Westminster, 1969.

McDonald, Lee Martin, and James Sanders. *The Canon Debate.* Peabody, Mass.: Hendrickson, 2002.

McKane, William. *Prophets and Wise Men.* London: SCM Press, 1965.

McKitterick, R. *The Uses of Literacy in Early Medieval Europe.* Cambridge: Cambridge University Press, 1990.

Melugin, Roy. "Amos in Recent Research." *Currents in Research: Biblical Studies* 6 (1998): 65–101.

Meynet, Roland. *Rhetorical Analysis: An Introduction to Biblical Rhetoric.* Sheffield: Sheffield Academic Press, 1998.

Moller, Karl. "'Hear This Word against You': A Fresh Look at the Arrangement and the Rhetorical Strategy of the Book of Amos." *Vetus Testamentum* 50 (2000): 499–518.

Mowinckle, Sigmund. *The Psalms in Israel's Worship.* 2 vols. Translated by D. Ap-Thomas. New York: Abingdon, 1962.

Murphy, Roland. *The Song of Songs* Minneapolis: Fortress, 1990.

Niditch, Susan. "The Composition of Isaiah 1." *Biblica* 6 (1980): 509–29.

———. *Oral World and Written Word.* Louisville, Ky.: Westminster John Knox, 1996.

Nissinen, Martti. *Prophecy in Its Ancient Near Eastern Context: Mesopotamian, Biblical, and Arabian Perspectives.* Atlanta: Society of Biblical Literature, 2000.

———. "Spoken, Written, Quoted, and Invented: Orality and Writtenness in Ancient Near Eastern Prophecy." Pages 235–72 in *Writings and Speech in Israelite and Ancient Near Eastern Prophecy.* Edited by Ehud Ben Zvi and Michael Floyd. Atlanta: Society of Biblical Literature, 2000.

Oesterreicher, Wulf. "Types of Orality in Text." Pages 190–214 in *Written Voices, Spoken Signs.* Edited by Egbert Bakker and Ahuvia Kahane. Cambridge, Mass.: Harvard University Press, 1997.

Ong, Walter J. *Orality and Literacy: The Technologizing of the Word*. New York: Methuen, 1982.

———. "Writing Is a Technology That Restructures Thought." Pages 23–50 in *The Written Word: Literacy in Transition*. Edited by Gerd Baumann. Oxford: Clarendon, 1986.

Overholt, Thomas W. "Prophecy: The Problem of Cross-Cultural Comparison." *Semeia* 21 (1982): 55–78.

———. *Prophecy in Cross-Cultural Perspective*. Atlanta: Scholars Press, 1986.

Paolucci, Anne and Henry, eds. *Hegel on Tragedy*. New York: Harper & Row, 1975.

Pattison, Robert. *On Literacy: The Politics of the Word from Homer to the Age of Rock*. Oxford: Oxford University Press, 1982.

Paul, Shalom. "Amos 1:3–2:3: A Concatenous Literary Pattern." *Journal of Biblical Literature* 40 (1971): 397–403.

———. *Amos*. Minneapolis: Fortress, 1991.

Peckham, Brian. *History and Prophecy: The Development of Late Judean Literary Traditions*. Anchor Bible Reference Library. New York: Doubleday, 1993.

Person, Raymond. "The Ancient Israelite Scribe as Performer." *Journal of Biblical Literature* 117 (1998): 601–9.

Peterson, David. "Basic Forms of Prophetic Literature." Pages 269–75 in *The Changing Face of Form Criticism for the Twenty-First Century*. Edited by Marvin Sweeney and Ehud Ben Zvi. Grand Rapids: Eerdmans, 2003.

———. "The Book of the Twelve / The Minor Prophets." Pages 95–128 in *The Hebrew Bible Today: An Introduction to Critical Issues*. Edited by S. L. McKenzie and M. Graham. Louisville, Ky.: Westminster John Knox, 1998.

———. *Prophecy in Israel*. Philadelphia: Fortress, 1987.

———. *Roles of Israel's Prophets*. Journal for the Study of the Old Testament: Supplement Series 17. Sheffield: Sheffield Academic Press, 1981.

Pfeifer, Gerhard. "Die Fremdvölkersprüche des Amos—spätere vaticinia ex eventu?" *Vetus Testamentum* 38 (1988): 230–33.

Pope, Marvin. *Song of Songs*. New York: Doubleday, 1977.

Reventlow, Graf. *Das Amt des Propheten bei Amos*. Göttingen: Vandenhoeck & Ruprecht, 1962.

Robinson, H. W. "Hebrew Sacrifice and Prophetic Symbolism." *Journal of Theological Studies* 43 (1942): 135–46.

Rottzoll, Dirk. *Studien zur Redaction und Komposition des Amosbuches*. Berlin: De Gruyter, 1996.

Rozik, Eli. "The Common Roots of Dreams and Theatre." *Assaph—Studies in the Theatre* 7 (1991): 75–102.

———. *The Ritual Roots of Theatre: Rethinking Ritual and Other Theories of Origin*. Iowa City: University of Iowa Press, 2002.

Schechner, Richard. *Between Theatre and Anthropology*. Philadelphia: University of Pennsylvania Press, 1985.

———. "Drama, Script, Theatre, and Performance." *Drama Review* 17, no. 3 (1973): 5–36.

Soggin, J. Alberto. "Amos and Wisdom." Pages 119–23 in *Wisdom in Ancient Israel*. Edited by J. Day et al. Cambridge: Cambridge University Press, 1995.

———. *The Prophet Amos: A Translation and Commentary*. Translated by J. Bowden. London: SCM Press, 1987.

Soll, Ludwig. *Gesprochenes und geschriebenes Französisch*. Berlin: Schmidt, 1985.

Sophocles. *The Three Theban Plays*. Translated by Robert Fagel. New York: Penguin, 1982.

Stacey, David. "The Function of Prophetic Drama." Pages 112–32 in *This Place Is Too Small for Us: The Israelite Prophets in Recent Scholarship*. Edited by R. Gordon. Winona Lake, Ind.: Eisenbrauns, 1995.

———. *Prophetic Drama in the Old Testament*. London: Epworth, 1990.

States, Bert O. *Great Reckonings in Little Rooms: On the Phenomenology of Theatre*. Berkeley: University of California Press, 1985.

———. "Performance as Metaphor." *Theatre Journal* 48, no. 1 (1996): 1–26.

Street, Brian. *Literacy in Theory and Practice*. Cambridge: Cambridge University Press, 1984.

Sweeney, Marvin, and Ehud Ben Zvi. *The Changing Face of Form Criticism for the Twenty-First Century*. Grand Rapids: Eerdmans, 2003.

Terrien, S. "Amos and Wisdom." *Israel's Prophetic Heritage*. Edited by B. W. Anderson and W. Harrelson. New York: Harper, 1962.

Thompson, Henry. *The Book of Amos: An Annotated Bibliography*. Lanham, Md.: Scarecrow, 1997.

Turkle, Sherry. "How Computers Change the Way We Think." *Chronicle of Higher Education*, January 30, 2004, section B, 26–28.

Uffenheimer, Benjamin. *Early Prophecy in Israel.* Jerusalem: Magnes, 1999.

Van den Born, A. *Profetie Metterdaad.* Roermond: Maaseik, 1947.

Wallace, Howard. *The Eden Narrative.* Atlanta: Scholars Press, 1985.

Ward, J. "The Eclipse of the Prophet in Contemporary Prophetic Studies." *Union Seminary Quarterly Review* 42 (1988): 97–104.

Weiser, Arthur. *Psalms.* Translated by Herbert Hartwell. Old Testament Library. Philadelphia: Westminster, 1962.

Wellhausen, Julius. *Prolegomena to the History of Israel.* Edinburgh: A&C Black, 1885.

Westermann, Claus. *Basic Forms of Prophetic Speech.* London: Lutterworth, 1967.

———. *Prophetic Oracles of Salvation in the Old Testament.* Louisville, Ky.: Westminster John Knox, 1991.

Wilson, Robert. "Prophets and Ecstasy: A Reexamination." *Journal of Biblical Literature* 98 (1979): 324–37.

Wise, Jennifer. *Dionysus Writes: The Invention of Theatre in Ancient Greece.* Ithaca, N.Y.: Cornell University Press, 1998.

Wolff, Hans Walter. *Amos the Prophet: The Man and His Background.* Translated by F. McCurley. Philadelphia: Fortress, 1973.

———. *Joel and Amos.* Translated by Waldemar Janzen, S. Dean McBride, and Charles Muenchow. Hermeneia. Philadelphia: Fortress, 1977.

Wood, Joyce Louise. "Amos: Prophecy as a Performing Art and Its Transformation in Book Culture." Ph.D. diss., St. Michael's College and Biblical Department of the Toronto School of Theology, 1993.

Wurthein, Ernst. "Amos-Studien." *Zeitschrift für die alttestamentliche Wissenschaft* 62 (1949–1950): 10–52.

Young, Ian. "Israelite Literacy: Interpreting the Evidence." *Vetus Testamentum* 48 (1998): 239–53.

SUBJECT INDEX

SCRIPTURE INDEX